LET'S ALL LEARN HOW TO FISH . . . TO SUSTAIN LONG-TERM ECONOMIC GROWTH

D1409096

Michael S. Falk, CFA

CFA Institute
Research
Foundation

Statement of Purpose

The CFA Institute Research Foundation is a not-for-profit organization established to promote the development and dissemination of relevant research for investment practitioners worldwide.

Cover Image Photo Credit: iStock.com/AlpamayoPhoto

ISBN 978-1-944960-05-6

May 2016

Editorial Staff

Elizabeth Collins
Editor

Abby Farson Pratt
Assistant Editor

Cindy Maisannes
Manager, Publications Technology
and Production

Tracy Dinning
Senior Publishing Technology Specialist

SUSTAINABLE FORESTRY INITIATIVE
Certified Sourcing
www.sfiprogram.org
SFI-01042

Biography

Michael S. Falk, CFA, is a partner at Focus Consulting, where he helps investment leaders leverage their talent. Previously, he was a chief strategist at Mauka Capital, LLC, a global macro hedge fund, and a chief investment officer in charge of manager due diligence and asset allocation for an advisory practice. Mr. Falk is part of the CFA Institute Approved Speaker List and teaches Claritas Program curriculum on behalf of CFA Society Chicago. He was a contributing member in the Financial Management Association's Practitioner Demand Driven Academic Research Initiative and served as an adjunct faculty member in the Certified Financial Planner certificate program at DePaul University. Mr. Falk is frequently quoted in the financial press and holds the Certified Retirement Counselor (CRC) designation.

Dedication

This book is dedicated to my wife and son. To my wife, Suzanne, thank you for all your love, support, patience, and understanding. And to my son, Collin, if only I can help make this world a better place for you . . .

Contents

Foreword ix
Preface xiii
Introduction: Let's All Learn How to Fish 1

Part I: Where Are We Now? **5**

1. Growth Challenges 6
   People (Number of Workers) 7
   Productivity 18
2. Entitlement to Responsibility with Appreciation (ERA) 28

Part II: What Could (Should) Be the Next ERA? **43**

3. Let's Retire Retirement (as we know it) 44
   First Principles for a Retirement Policy 49
   Today's Retirement Planning To-Do's (if you must) 61
4. A Cure for Health Care 67
   First Principles for Health Care Policy 68
   Today's Health To-Do's (because you should) 87
5. Learn to Learn (and never stop) 90
   First Principles for the Educational System 95
   Today's Educational To-Do's (learn 'em, love 'em, live 'em) 105

Conclusion: It Is Time for a New ERA of Sustainable Growth 109
Appendix 1. Taxes 113
Appendix 2. Dealing with Underfunded Public Pension Plans 115
References 117

CE Qualified Activity ⚛ **CFA Institute** — This publication qualifies for 5 CE credits under the guidelines of the CFA Institute Continuing Education Program.

Foreword

The bad economist sees only what immediately strikes the eye; the good economist also looks beyond. The bad economist sees only the direct consequences of a proposed course; the good economist looks also at the longer and indirect consequences. The bad economist sees only what the effect of a given policy has been or will be on one particular group; the good economist inquires also what the effect of the policy will be on all groups.

—*Henry Hazlitt,* Economics in One Lesson, *1946*

Not a day goes by without us hearing how miserable the state of the economy is. It is not really true—more people are living far above subsistence than at any other time in the history of the world—but a lot of things do need improvement. Poverty is and, seemingly, always will be with us. Governments are stretched to their limits in providing services that the people demand but will not or cannot pay for. The environment and infrastructure present long-term challenges.

Much of this misery is the result of bad policies. Some of the policies are well intentioned and arise from what author and entrepreneur Gary Hoover calls "misguided sympathy."[1] They are designed to help people but destroy incentives to work and replace them with incentives to draw on the fruits of others' labor. Other policies are less well intentioned and are designed to help only those people pursuing the policies; economists call this practice "rent seeking." Enough misguided sympathy and rent seeking and you can destroy an economy and a civilization. We are not there yet, and we had better not get there.

In the 1940s, the great economic journalist Henry Hazlitt drew a distinction between good and bad economics. He said that bad economics is characterized by

- confusing the intended with the unintended consequences of a policy,

- focusing on the consequences of a policy for one group and ignoring the consequences for other groups, and

- confusing the short-run with the long-run consequences of an action.

These errors are the source of much trouble and are the main reason bad public policies exist. People invoke the power of government to try to help some

---

[1]Gary E. Hoover, "Who Is to Blame for the Chicago Ghetto?" *Hoover's World* (2009): http://hooversworld.com/who-is-to-blame-for-the-chicago-ghetto.

specific group; the help does not help (the actual consequences are mistaken for the intended ones, Hazlitt's first point) and makes the situation worse.

Not seeing the connection between the help and the damage, the helpers often redouble their efforts and thus compound the damage. The damage spreads to people who were initially unaffected (Hazlitt's second point).

The newly damaged group then cries out for help, closing the circle (the long-run consequences differ from the short-run, Hazlitt's third point). Thus, government not only fails to achieve its goals but also grows ever more costly over time.

This circle can be broken. People respond to incentives—the economist Steven Landsburg has written that all of economics can be summed up in those four words[2]—so, let's set up incentives for people to produce more. In *Let's All Learn How to Fish*, Michael Falk, an investment manager and consultant, shows how a more productive society can be organized around well-designed incentives to succeed and safety nets—accompanied by "trampolines"—to protect those who fail and to help them regain entry into the world of work and enterprise. As this virtuous cycle proceeds, not only do tax revenues rise and needs fall, but people also become healthier and happier.

This book is not a left-wing or a right-wing treatise. It advocates for a social safety net at the same time that it asks us to embrace self-reliance. Self-reliance has taken on a conservative hue recently, but its most eloquent exponent, Ralph Waldo Emerson, was one of the 19th century's greatest liberals. In fact, if *Let's All Learn How to Fish* must be classified, it is as a liberal book—exalting the dignity of the individual above all other values and calling on the community to support that dignity.

Calvin Coolidge extolled the virtue of economic self-reliance in his first and only inaugural address:

> I favor the policy of economy, not because I wish to save money, but because I wish to save people. The men and women of this country who toil are the ones who bear the cost of . . . government. Every dollar that we carelessly waste means that their life will be so much the more meager. Every dollar that we prudently save means that their life will be so much the more abundant. Economy is idealism in its most practical form.

It is in this spirit that we must all try to learn how to fish. Some of us, and every one of us at some time in our lives, will not be able to fish. We all know this fact and must allow for it. We cannot completely avoid drawing on each other's resources as our talent, energy, and good fortune wax and wane.

---

[2]Steven E. Landsburg, *The Armchair Economist: Economics & Everyday Life* (New York: Free Press, 2012). The first sentences of the book are, "Most of economics can be summarized in four words: 'People respond to incentives.' The rest is commentary."

President Coolidge's observation is a good way to think about modulating the impulse to reach into each other's pockets. We have to rely on others sometimes; as Supreme Court Justice Oliver Wendell Holmes, Jr., said, taxes are the price of civilization. But he did not say how high the price should be, so we should constantly remind ourselves to rely on others sparingly.

Let's All Learn How to Fish provides realistic suggestions for a society that cherishes the value of the individual and the spirit of humane generosity while making sure that we do not exhaust each other's resources. By publishing this excellent and provocative monograph, the CFA Institute Research Foundation takes a direction different from the usual. I cannot think of a better way to seek out new ground.

Laurence B. Siegel
Gary P. Brinson Director of Research
CFA Institute Research Foundation
March 2016

Preface

While you read this book, please keep in mind the following quotation from Carveth Read: "It is better to be vaguely right than exactly wrong."[3]

Because this book references a great deal of data and data can be interpreted in many ways, I caution that some of the conclusions, if not all of them, are best when tempered. Deirdre Nansen McCloskey has written, "One of the problems is the very word *data*, meaning 'things given': scientists should deal in *capta*, 'things seized.'" In this regard, I have "capta'd" many things from many others and would like to acknowledge their contributions. Isaac Newton once wrote, "If I have seen further, it is by standing on the shoulders of giants."[4] I have the utmost gratitude to and appreciation for the shoulders on which I have stood. Thank you to

- Jerry Falk, my father, for the values he instilled in me; I am a better person because of him;

- my partners at Focus Consulting Group for how they help to bolster my mastery of working with, relating to, and understanding people as well as how they continue to challenge me to be better;

- my partner from Mauka Capital, LLC, for all of the wonderfully wandering investment and economic dialogues about the world and all its interconnectedness;

- the original Financial Management Association's Practitioner Demand Driven Academic Research Initiative (PDDARI) "gang" for their confidence and long-term interest in my views; in particular, thank you to PDDARI's Lee Hayes, CFA, for his input and discussion of this book; and

- the many researchers, writers, and industry experts who have pushed my thinking with their words and publications.

I would also like to thank the CFA Institute Research Foundation and Larry Siegel, the Gary P. Brinson director of research, for their willingness to publish my "straw man" ideas to start what I hope will be a proper and productive dialogue.

---

[3]Carveth Read, *Logic: Deductive and Inductive* (London: Grant Richards, 1898). A similar quotation is often attributed to John Maynard Keynes but not sourced: "It is better to be roughly right than precisely wrong."

[4]In a letter to Robert Hooke (5 February 1676).

Introduction: Let's All Learn How to Fish

> Give a person a fish and you feed him or her for a day; teach a person to fish and you feed him or her for a lifetime.
>
> *—Author's paraphrase of a proverb attributed to Maimonides (1135–1204)*

For all of us, economic health and economic growth are heavily influenced by social policies on entitlements, government spending, taxation, and personal incentives—in particular, how we are motivated and what we are required to share with others. Have we taught too few individuals how to fish for themselves and handed out too many fish?

The following maxim, which has been attributed to Mahatma Gandhi, may be true—"a nation's greatness is measured by how it treats its weakest members." That is, for those who are unable to learn or no longer capable of fishing, let's strive for this view of greatness and offer proper safety nets. According to Rajan and Zingales (2003), "A safety net is . . . a mechanism to ensure political consensus for free markets . . . it is also a way to encourage people to invest in their future"—that is, save for their future. But well-intentioned policies may not only fail to achieve greatness but also conspire to defeat it. Well-intentioned but poorly designed or implemented incentives pose real risks to a prosperous economic future. Let's promote and support quality education and health care—and then, go fish.

The growth rate of an economy depends on many factors. In the "national income accounting" approach used in the United States, the growth rate is numerically equal to the percentage change in real output per worker (called "productivity") plus the percentage change in the number of workers.[5] Incentives that negatively affect (even unintentionally) either variable—workers or productivity—lower economic growth. For example, a 10% decrease in the number of workers (which is a forecast for the United States between now and 2020) would require productivity growth of at least 10% in total over that period for real economic growth of *zero* to be maintained. To achieve a 3% GDP growth rate, often described as the rate consistent with a healthy

---

[5]This accounting identity is true by construction, but there are other ways to decompose GDP growth. The "total factor productivity" approach, attributable to Solow (1996), may be more revealing because it accounts for the separate contributions of land (including natural resources), labor, capital, and entrepreneurship. Another approach focuses on technology; it essentially ascribes all improvements in productivity to changes in technology, broadly defined. Throughout this book, "productivity" is used to mean *real output per worker* unless another definition is stated.

economy, productivity would have to grow much faster than 3% per year. Modern history has shown that 3% productivity growth (for most developed countries) is extremely difficult to achieve. A 3% growth rate was a high hurdle even in the past, when the shifts in economic activity were less frequent and less significant than they have been in recent decades. If the recent global shifts from industrial to service-based economies continue, then maintaining a 3% productivity growth rate will likely become an even greater challenge.

Policies that create incentives for retirement, employment, migration, fertility, and family formation affect the size of current and potential worker populations. In developed economies, the current custom of retiring at or near the age of 65 was based on two premises that are no longer valid. First, in agrarian and industrial economies—where retirement as a policy was born—older individuals may have had little if any productive capacity beyond a certain age. In today's service-based economy, however, that is much less true. Second, the exit of everyone over 65 from the workforce was sustainable when the dependency ratio—that is, the population ratio of workers to retired individuals—was about 20 to 1. This ratio, which was typical of an agrarian society in the early to mid-20th century, is no longer sustainable. Today, the dependency ratio—based on global life expectancies, fertility rates, productivity rate projections, and the changed physical nature of work in developed economies—is closer to 3 to 1 and projected to shrink toward 2 to 1 in this author's lifetime. Yesterday's age 65 is estimated to be roughly age 73 today.[6]

Policies and costs that alter the value propositions of health insurance, education, and capital investments affect productivity. For example, among the myriad issues with health insurance coverage, we know that when a user of services is someone other than the payer for services, resources are expensively misallocated. One must also ask to what extent, if at all, health care is a right and, as a result, if resource misallocations are simply a price to be paid. The United States is a particularly stark example of misallocation of resources. The United States spends roughly 2.5 times as much per capita on the delivery of health services compared with the OECD average based on 2013 purchasing power parity data but has not demonstrated better outcomes in terms of increased longevity or decreased infant mortality than most other developed economies (OECD 2015).

The pain of much slower economic growth can be avoided with better policies. And in these indebted times, higher growth rates are crucial. Unfortunately, policy discussions that include entitlements, government spending, or taxation degenerate into bitter arguments used to bolster political agendas. The goal of this book is to enable constructive dialogue on these

---

[6]See Arnott and Casscells (2003), Saletan (2005), and Shoven (2009).

issues through an honest attempt to understand today's policies in terms of where we are now, what policies could be next, and where we need to go to sustain long-term economic growth.

I have intentionally and purposefully built this global straw man of policy principles on the basis of my experiences, views, and research. Please consider carefully these ideas and principles before you strike your match. And remember that, although Descartes gave us "I think, therefore I am," Saint Augustine gave us "I err, therefore I am" long before Descartes.

When reading this book, know that my heart preceded my mind in this effort. I have a child and someday hope for a grandchild or grandchildren. I believe personal responsibility is important and dictates that we should consider future generations and do no harm. And I hope you follow that same path. You may not agree with all of my conclusions, which is perfectly acceptable because my purpose is to bring ideas forward to foster a proper dialogue.

Part I: Where Are We Now?

In Part I, I explore the primary challenges to economic growth and prosperity through an examination of people and productivity. Then, I make a case for a new era in which individuals appreciate what they have or have been given and take responsibility for themselves and those in need of help.

1. Growth Challenges

Without continual growth and progress, such words as improvement, achievement, and success have no meaning.

—Attributed to Benjamin Franklin

Do you believe that we will run out of fish? Or do you think we can manage the supply of fish in a sustainable manner? The economic growth of the past couple of centuries has accomplished some wonderful things for the citizenry of the world. Many people now worry, however, about whether our aging global economies can produce enough growth to overcome the massive debts accumulated and the even larger future liabilities, the "promises" made to current generations. What about the need to preserve hope for young people and for generations not yet born? Should not these generations have the same opportunities as their predecessors did? To put the future—with regard to aging and its associated liabilities—into perspective, how do you mentally process the International Monetary Fund (IMF) report (2009) on the whopping age-related costs as compared with the recent Great Recession costs, as shown in **Figure 1**?

Perhaps a multiple choice question would be helpful? The impact of the IMF forecast on me is:

a. Immaterial. I will be long dead by 2050 (and I do not care about future generations).

Figure 1. Net Present Value of Impact of Fiscal Deficit of 2008 Crisis and Age-Related Spending to 2050
(% of GDP)

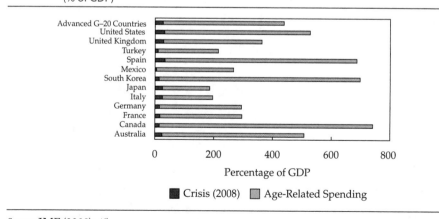

Source: IMF (2009): 45.

b. Immaterial. Herbert Stein (1998) was right: "If something cannot go on forever, it will stop." So, we will never pay for such impossible-to-support liabilities.

c. Immaterial. C'mon, the IMF and economic forecasts? Alfred E. Neuman was spot on: "What, me worry?"

d. Material. Oh, \$#^!, what can I do for my family and myself to prepare?

e. Material. We (all) need to work together and change our policies to get off of this path NOW!

Exhibit 1 lists the respective primary drivers that affect economic growth. The importance of today's policies cannot be overstated; the incentives—intended or otherwise—pose challenges to economic growth and its effect on all of us. The liability side will also greatly affect future generations—and may do irreparable harm. These factors consider people, their productivity, government-styled promises, and the prospects for growth.

Policies that shrink worker populations or restrict productive capacity seem inadvisable on their face, but is that not generally what many developed-world policies accomplish? I will review the current state of growth prospects as it relates to these factors.

People (Number of Workers)

The following is an exploration of the four factors that have the greatest effects on the number of workers: retirement, employment (or the participation of people in the workforce), net migration, and fertility.

Retirement. A sensible retirement policy must balance the declining ability of people to work against the value of human capital that persists into older ages. Consider that retirement, as a concept, is quite young; it dates back to the late 19th century and is based on the concept that older workers will have primarily, if not completely, used up their human capital by their 60s. That concept

Exhibit 1. Primary Factors Affecting Economic Growth

Effects on the Number of Workers	Effects on the Amount of Productivity
• Retirement	• Health
• Employment/participation	• Education/skill relevancy
• Net migration	• Investment capital
• Fertility	

may be accurate in agrarian economies because of the physical difficulty of the work, but it is less true in manufacturing economies and is mostly inaccurate in service-based economies. Today's world economy is less dependent on human labor in agriculture than in the past and is tending away from Thomas Hobbes's statement that "the life of man [is] solitary, poor, nasty, brutish, and short."[7] **Figure 2** demonstrates this trend for the United States.

Have you ever thought of retirement policy as an incentive to leave the workforce and reduce its size? That was the intention, in part, to manipulate unemployment statistics to make the economy appear healthier than it was because unemployed workers above a certain age were no longer considered unemployed. At the time, this assumption held because more than half of people did not live to the 60–65 retirement age, and of those who did, many died shortly thereafter, so the social cost of retirement was small.

Today, more and more people live until retirement and for many years beyond—this is *good*. The founder of the International Longevity Center, Robert N. Butler, perhaps said it best when he noted that it is a "terrible waste of talent to have [retirees] sitting idly for 20 or 30 years."[8]

The growing population of older individuals in need of support, however, results in ever-increasing social costs. Retirement policy detracts from growth insofar as governments are the primary source of retirement income.

---

[7]Thomas Hobbes, *Leviathan* (London: 1651).
[8]See http://castle.eiu.edu/~lsimpson/fcs5301/Stereoptypes/ElderWeb.htm.

Figure 2.   Sector Composition of US and Europe Employment over Time

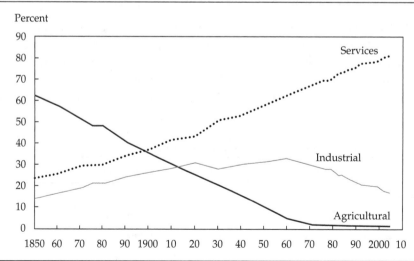

Source: Inklaar, Timmer, and Van Ark (2008).

Supporting retirees diverts funds to consumption and from other uses. Those government revenues cannot be reinvested back into society or are likely to be invested privately by the retirees. According to a 2014 article in the *Economist*: "Under the UN's standard assumption that a working life ends at 65, and with no increases in productivity, ageing populations could cut growth rates in parts of the rich world by between one-third and one-half over the coming years" ("Age Invaders" 2014).

Individuals could voluntarily work longer, but they do not have much incentive to do so. Policies need to change to help create an incentive for later retirement (thus increased overall production).

Employment/Participation. All able-bodied or able-minded individuals who are part of a workforce help economic growth, but school-aged children, retired individuals, and other able-bodied and able-minded individuals who are not part of the workforce detract from growth. Such trends as students staying in school longer and workers taking early retirement intensify the challenge. There is both the loss of the available human capital and the cost from well-intentioned unemployment "nets."

In 2016, good jobs may be scarce, but the unemployment nets might also be too broad and seductive to encourage workers to take less-than-ideal jobs. If nonwork is (too) "comfortable," workforce participation declines. In the United States, the falling labor participation rate, as shown in **Figure 3**, is worrisome.

Safety nets are clearly a factor. For example, according to David Autor, the Social Security Disability Insurance program "creates a very strong incentive

Figure 3. US Labor Force Participation Rate, 1985–2015 (November)

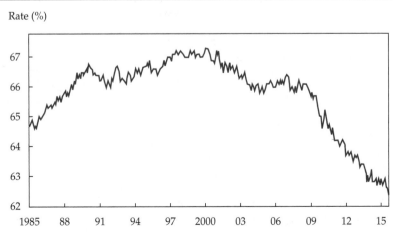

Source: US Bureau of Labor Statistics.

against meaningfully participating in the formal labor market" (Epstein 2014). As **Figure 4** shows, the share of men and women ages 25–54 and 55–64 receiving disability payments from the Social Security Administration has soared over the past few decades, hurting the workforce participation rate. A sharp rise in disability claims among older individuals, who may no longer wish to work, is probably evidence of an incentives problem.

On the one hand, too few safety nets drive savings rates higher, as seen in some countries in Asia. On the other hand, high savings rates can be negative for growth. Sadly, mismatches between preexisting skills and job opportunities will always contribute to this challenge; unemployment will happen. The best approach may be to consider what constitutes a *responsible* duration of unemployment. "Responsible" is a fair term because of the lost human capital potential that occurs in a society when masses of people go into the unemployment safety net. When one considers that the value of human capital (in the United States) has been estimated at 5–10 times that of physical capital, the size of the loss becomes evident (Jorgenson and Fraumeni 1989).

In general, we could all benefit from the use of more trampolines (a combination of benefits and work requirements) to help people bounce back rather than just rely on nets. Unemployment could and should be used to start a new business (i.e., a person could fully embrace responsibility), obtain the needed education or new skills to restart a career, or relocate to where a suitable job exists. At a minimum, those who are unemployed could be expected to leverage

Figure 4. Disability Explosion

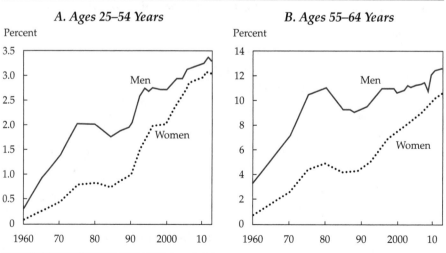

Source: Social Security Administration.

someone else's human capital via caring for their young or elderly family members. Perhaps the responsible duration question should be reframed as: How long does it take to start, obtain, acquire, or relocate—SOAR—again? If policies began to include and require the use of trampolines in addition to the existing nets, we could enable more workers to actually work. In this book, I will share policy perspectives oriented toward trampolines.

If a proper expectation is to have people work beyond their 60s, then we should expect that individuals will have multiple careers. Early careers might be more physical in nature, whereas later careers should be less physical. Individuals who have developed specific expertise might migrate to positions that transfer their specific knowledge to others rather than doing the work. Disability policies need to reflect this reality. Many individuals defined as disabled may need to go through a transition similar to that of unemployment because most medical conditions do not result in total disability.

Net Migration. It almost goes without saying that an economy can benefit from migration, both domestic and international. Here, I focus on *immigration* into the United States.

In 1883, Emma Lazarus wrote, "Give me your tired, your poor, your huddled masses yearning to breathe free . . ." and the United States welcomed immigrants. Today, it seems that in the United States and many other developed countries, the masses have become largely unwelcome. This change is ironic because immigration has provided both the United States and Western Europe with large boosts to growth over time (OECD 2014). Arguments against immigration today vary: Immigrants will take our jobs (maybe, but is it true because of them or you?). They will lower our wages (maybe, but why should your wages be safe anyway?). They will live off our government (which is not their fault but ours for allowing our government to offer social nets that "catch" more than designed).[9] Unfortunately, such arguments are often simply the ugly face of xenophobia.

To the extent that the research is clear, a country should have, at a minimum, no restrictions on educated, hard-working, and law-abiding individuals immigrating. In fact, according to Professor Giovanni Peri, "College-educated workers are much more mobile than less educated ones, and they move to

[9]Razin and Sadka (2014) write, "European welfare and migration policies are strikingly different from states within the US. Over the last half century, Europe ended up with 85% of all unskilled migrants to developed countries, whereas the US retains its innovative edge by attracting 55% of the world-educated migrants... The ageing of the population affects the political power balance, and thereby the generosity of the welfare state and its migration policies. A more aged society would naturally entail more political influence for the old who opt for a more generous welfare state. On the other hand, the working young, who finance the welfare state, are more reluctant to increase its generosity" (www.voxeu.org/article/migration-and-welfare-us-and-europe).

countries where they are better paid . . . Hence immigration tends to reduce wage differentials between the lowest and the highest paid workers in receiving countries . . . educated people are job-creating and complement less educated, local workers in productive activities. Emigration does the opposite."[10]

Consider **Figure 5**, which is based on educated migrants who hold patents. Simply put, a country that welcomes immigrants—those who want to work—can increase its number of workers. Bigger, younger working populations aid growth. Therefore, entrepreneurs who have funding should perhaps consider "start-up" visas as a complement to an increase in H1B visas.[11] Such a system exists today, to some degree, in Australia, the United Kingdom, Chile, and Canada.

Nevertheless, immigration is close to, but not fully, a zero-sum game, and not all economies can be winners.[12] Is your country a desired destina-

---

[10]See www.res.org.uk/details/mediabrief/6788651/IMMIGRATION-BOOSTS-THE-PAY-OF-LESS-EDUCATED-NATIVES-EMIGRATION-DOES-THE-OPPOSITE.html.
[11]The H1B visa is a nonimmigrant visa designed to allow US employers to recruit and employ foreign professionals in specialty occupations within the United States for a specified period of time.
[12]Note, for example, that Ireland in the 1840s could be considered better off after more than 1 million people left because the remaining population then had enough food.

Figure 5. Inventor Immigrants and Emigrants

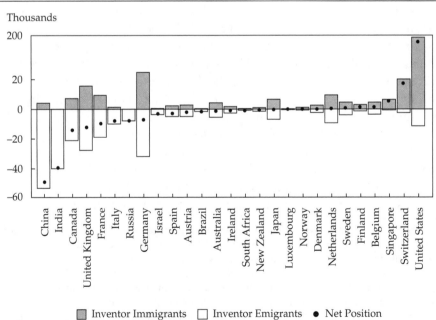

Source: Fink, Miguelez, and Raffo (2013).

tion that welcomes immigrants? **Table 1** shows the top seven countries people immigrate to when seeking jobs.

Strack (2014), the source of Table 1, also investigated why people emigrate. Those who moved across national borders in search of better job opportunities looked for these attributes: (1) appreciation for their work, (2) good relationships with colleagues, (3) good work/life balance, and (4) good relationships with superiors. For those who are curious, an attractive salary was ranked eighth.

Table 1. Mobility Based on 200,000 Workers

	Most Preferred Country of Immigration
Rank	Percentage
1. United States	42%
2. United Kingdom	37
3. Canada	35
4. Germany	33
5. Switzerland	29
6. France	29
7. Australia	28

Note: The table shows the most preferred country of immigration according to residents from the top 24 countries with the highest levels of emigration.
Source: Strack (2014).

Fertility. The most fundamental driver behind the potential number of workers is the number of people born in a society, who will, in time, become the workers. Fertility data are a major reason why demography is often described as destiny; in an age when early death is uncommon, the number of people born is by far the primary determinant of the number of people in each age group later on. So, what do demographic forecasts tell us about our future labor needs? **Figure 6** shows that [from table] total fertility rates declined in all regions between 1970 and 2013. Fertility rates have been dropping everywhere. The replacement rate, or fertility rate that stabilizes a developed population's growth, is 2.1 children per woman; in developing societies, where higher levels of infant mortality and female deaths before the age of reproduction are more common, the replacement rate is estimated to be 2.7 children per woman.

The replacement rate statistics hide materially unbalanced male-to-female births found in some countries (e.g., China's 118 male births to every 100 female births), which negatively affect fertility rate expectations. Fertility

Figure 6. Total Fertility Rates by Region, 1970 vs. 2013

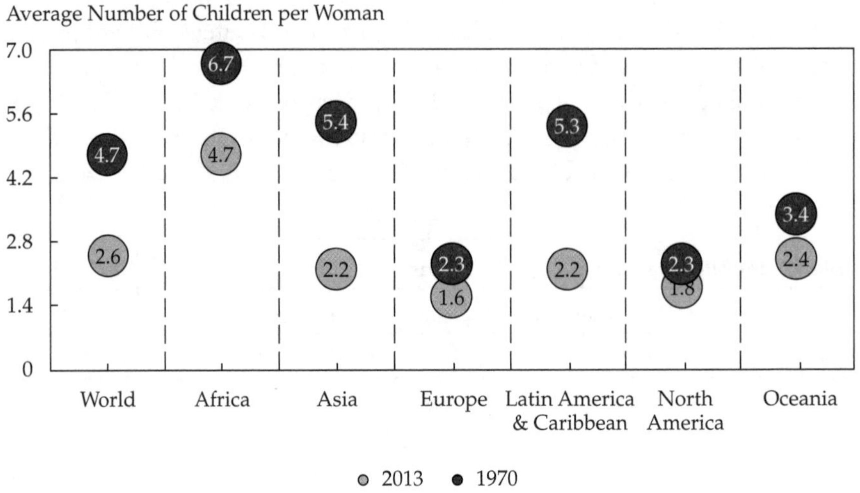

Average Number of Children per Woman

Source: Haub and Kaneda (2014).

rates together with economic growth projections can help highlight the potential employment picture in the future. **Table 2** shows that labor shortages are likely in developed countries.

This trend is certainly not good news to countries that need more people to support more growth. Those robots that threaten some jobs just may be the solution.

Note that the numbers in Table 2 are averages, so shortages of highly skilled workers could be worse than the table suggests. Moreover, the mismatch could worsen with technological progress because the ratio of less skilled workers or detached highly skilled workers to skilled workers could also accelerate. Low-skilled jobs are not the types of jobs that are needed to increase society's overall productivity.[13] (Of course, this situation quickly brings to mind the obvious question as to why infrastructure jobs are not vigorously pursued to employ younger or less formally educated workers.)

Skills and jobs aside, could fertility rates in the developed world rebound and eliminate the coming labor shortage? Here's why that's not likely:

---

[13]A typical reason given is that governance (governments, unions) is so poor on these projects that citizenry might pay several times the going rate for the infrastructure and the infrastructure might never be built. This issue could be overcome, however, with disclosed bidding processes, independent selection committees, the blinding of the bidders to the selectors, and/or the addition of price incentives for timing and/or quality metrics.

Table 2. Labor Shortages and Surpluses by Country, 2020 and 2030

Country	2020 (% of labor supply)		2030 (% of labor supply)	
	Scenario 1 (10-year growth rate)	Scenario 2 (20-year growth rate)	Scenario 1 (10-year growth rate)	Scenario 2 (20-year growth rate)
Europe				
France	8	6	5	–1
Germany	–6	–4	–27	–23
Italy	8	8	–4	–4
Netherlands	14	10	5	–7
Poland	–1	5	–24	–10
Spain	24	17	16	–3
Sweden	7	9	4	8
Switzerland	–9	–5	–19	–10
United Kingdom	8	6	3	–1
Americas				
Argentina	3	24	–23	30
Brazil	–7	–7	–34	–33
Canada	5	3	–6	–11
Mexico	10	6	4	–8
United States	13	10	11	4
Asia Pacific				
Australia	–3	–2	–18	–16
China	9	7	3	–3
India	8	6	4	1
Indonesia	3	5	–3	0
Japan	3	3	–2	–2
Russia	–5	11	–24	15
Saudi Arabia	16	30	–19	20
South Korea	–2	–6	–16	–26
Turkey	7	8	0	4
Africa				
Egypt	7	9	–5	0
South Africa	30	36	26	39

Notes: No color in cell = surplus; light gray cell = de facto shortage (i.e., surplus of 0%–5%); black cell = shortage. Surplus or shortage = Labor supply – Labor demand. Scenarios are based on 10-year or 20-year compound annual growth rates (CAGRs) of GDP and productivity. For Russia, the 10-year scenario is more realistic than the 20-year scenario. Poland's labor productivity CAGR is based on 1996–2012; Saudi Arabia's, 2000–2012; and South Africa's, 2001–2012.
Source: Strack (2014).

1. Until the 1960s, improved longevity was mostly a result of the decreased mortality of infants—ages 0–3—in the averages. This great news was a result of improvements in sanitation, medical care, and education. The natural reaction to the decrease in this mortality was a decreased need for more children, what some refer to as "spares" (see Oeppen and Vaupel 2002).

2. The move away from agrarian economies reduces the need for labor—specifically children, who serve as free laborers. (In reality, nothing is free. The children have a cost, but the labor of children is often perceived as free, and it is perception that drives behavior.)

3. Increases in per capita wealth have been shown to reduce fertility. In fact, as **Figure 7** shows, there is a strong, inverse correlation between income and number of children.

4. People have begun to marry later or not at all. The result has been fewer children. And since 2000, joblessness and indebtedness (college and

Figure 7. Correlation between Income and Fertility, 2013

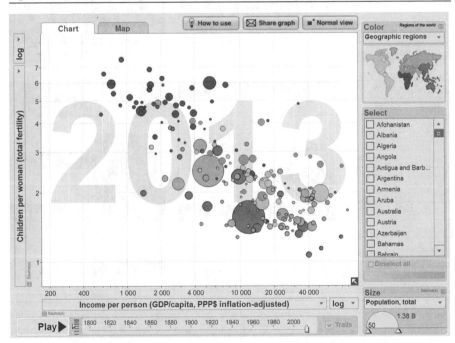

Note: To view the labels and interact with this figure, please visit www.bit.ly/1OtrKsj.
Sources: World Bank, UN Population Division, and Gapminder.org.

postcollege debts) have retarded family formation. Although this last trend is not long term, it is worrisome and should be watched.

The top three explanations seem to be (1) parents no longer need or expect their children to support them in old age; (2) according to Ramey (2009), people believe that the combination of fewer kids and greater resources per child will produce "better" kids (if not better lives for the parents); and (3) economic development and urbanization tends to mix people together and change mating patterns.[14]

In aggregate, then, policies regarding the worker side of the economic growth equation do not instill much confidence in or hope for growth. This situation has led to such statements as, "The entitlements problem is not a financial problem exacerbated by a failure to prefund these obligations but, rather, is a support ratio problem tied to demography, pure and simple" (Arnott and Chaves 2012, p. 25). Specifically and globally, Manyika et al. (2015) stated,

> The problem is that slower population growth and longer life expectancy are limiting growth in the working-age population. For the past half century, the twin engines of rapid population growth (expanding the number of workers) and a brisk increase in labor productivity powered the expansion of gross domestic product. Employment and productivity grew at compound annual rates of 1.7 percent and 1.8 percent, respectively, between 1964 and 2014, pushing the output of an average employee 2.4 times higher. Yet this demographic tailwind is weakening and even becoming a headwind in many countries.

> The net result is that employment will grow by just 0.3 percent annually during the next 50 years, forecasts a new report from the McKinsey Global Institute (MGI)—Global growth: Can productivity save the day in an aging world? Even if productivity growth matches its rapid rate during the past half century, the rate of increase in global GDP growth will therefore still fall by 40 percent, to about 2.1 percent a year.

The good news is that there is considerable potential for improvement in work spans and immigration policies.

Without substantial, successful changes to policies (e.g., retirement age eligibility, immigration, labor force participation), the productivity side of the growth equation will need to carry the burden of growth and become much more robust than it has ever been in the past. So, what are the prospects for productivity growth?

---

[14]Some research suggests that the mixing of people from different backgrounds in cities reduces total fertility, even after controlling for other factors. See, for example, Helgason et al. (2008).

Productivity

Productivity growth is a measure of increases in efficiency and can be thought of simply as the ability to get more from less. An amusing counterexample, illustrating how *not* to grow productivity, was provided by Milton Friedman, as recalled by the *Wall Street Journal* editorial page editor Stephen Moore (2009):

> At one of our dinners, Milton recalled traveling to an Asian country in the 1960s and visiting a worksite where a new canal was being built. He was shocked to see that, instead of modern tractors and earth movers, the workers had shovels. He asked why there were so few machines. The government bureaucrat explained: "You don't understand. This is a jobs program." To which Milton replied: "Oh, I thought you were trying to build a canal. If it's jobs you want, then you should give these workers spoons, not shovels."

One cannot boost production (i.e., boost GDP) merely by boosting the amount of effort expended. The effort has to be sensible and efficient; otherwise, the effect is to take away from, rather than increase, the stock of resources produced. But moving to more efficient productive processes—that is, increasing productivity—has a downside. Think of business owners who use modern machinery to replace dozens of people wielding shovels (or thousands wielding spoons!), and then consider the pattern shown in **Figure 8** of US median family real income as productivity increases.

Figure 8. Wage Gap: US Productivity and Median Family Income, 1945–2014

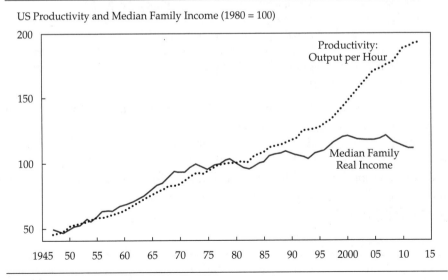

US Productivity and Median Family Income (1980 = 100)

Source: Mian and Sufi (2014).

At first glance, the substitution of capital for labor does not appear to be an attractive trade-off. What are all of the unemployed workers supposed to do? This analysis is static, however (what is the consequence of a given action at a moment in time?), when it should be dynamic (what is the consequence over time?). Over time, some workers develop new skills to adapt to the higher productivity, higher wage environment; others drop out of the workforce. The net effect, historically, has been positive when summed across workers, although not necessarily positive for any given worker—or given country, for that matter. Consider the trade-off in time/productivity versus jobs in the picture shown in **Figure 9**.

Clearly, bricklaying jobs will be lost. But who made the machine? Who made the machines that were used to make the machine? Who found or mined or processed the natural resources that went into making the machines? In this regard, Frédéric Bastiat argued that people react to benefits and costs that they can see—the lost bricklaying jobs—but not to benefits and costs that they cannot see.[15] Figure 9 is what is seen (a road-laying machine and, eventually, a road) but behind it is what is unseen (e.g., lower road taxes, better

---

[15]Bastiat (1801–1850) was a French economist, legislator, and writer who championed private property, free markets, and limited government.

Figure 9. Bricklaying Machine

Source: Tiger-Stone.

roads that shorten people's commutes and increase productivity, wealthier machine designers and manufacturers, poorer bricklayers, richer steelworkers). Furthermore, those who profit from a machine may reside in another country. Offsets are rarely balanced, even when positive.

The topic, then, is complex; both Friedman's simplified story and today's inequality debates fail to do it justice. Today, financial and physical capital formation, on the one hand, and human capital formation, on the other hand, are encouraged differently through regulation, taxation, and benefits (or entitlements). Productivity growth is not the enemy, nor should it be restrained; it is the correct goal. After all, it is the way people in general have been able to raise living standards over the past couple of centuries. It is also the way everyone might be able to overcome the slow growth expectations brought on by the leveling off of population.

Back in 1956, Robert Solow (who would go on to win the Nobel Prize in 1987) wrote, "Let us agree to count as growth-promoting any act that permanently enlarges the stock of tangible capital, or human capital, or knowledge capital, in the sense that it causes the stock of capital to be forever larger than it would have been if that act had not occurred" (p. 300). Research on the topic has expanded materially since this quotation. So, let's review the three main levers that most affect the size of our permanent stock of capital—health, education and skill relevancy, and investment capital.

Health. Productivity growth is directly affected by the health of the workforce. Positive changes in morbidity (i.e., reduced sickness, fewer work days missed because of injury or illness) and healthy aging rather than simply improved longevity (i.e., more total work done because of improved vigor) can be significantly additive. Although health expenditures can increase productive capacities, health care expenditures also reduce the amount of capital that can be invested elsewhere. Economic growth suffers (because of the cost expended) when health care expenditures do not decrease morbidity or increase healthy aging.

The state of health care policies and behaviors today offers real potential for improvement. For example, the estimated global GDP costs of obesity are now nearly the same as those of smoking, while both continue to show harmful trends (Dobbs et al. 2014). A potential game changer, according to author, computer scientist, inventor, and futurist Ray Kurzweil, is the ability to switch off our fat cells. He wrote:

> Thanks to the Human Genome Project, medicine is now information technology, and we're learning how to reprogram this outdated software of our bodies exponentially. In animals with diabetes, scientists have now

successfully turned off the fat insulin receptor gene. So these animals ate ravenously, remained slim, didn't get diabetes, and lived 20 per cent longer. I would say that this will be a human intervention in 5 to 10 years (2020), and we will have the means of really controlling our weight independent of our eating. ("How the World Will Change")

Whether or not this promise will be realized, the productivity potential in new health-related technologies and services offers reason for real optimism. Based in part on the increase in the knowledge of genetic processes that has occurred since the Human Genome Project, health care advances can be expected to continue to yield productivity gains.

There's also great potential for policies that could create incentives for better health-related behavior involving greater personal responsibility. After all, "70% of our chronic health care costs are occasioned by the abuse of alcohol and other substances (especially tobacco!), physical inactivity, poor food choices and overly generous portion sizes, and unmanaged stress. We could avoid a substantial fraction of these costs if people had better incentives to make lifestyle changes and were able to change their behavior."[16]

Education and Skill Relevancy. Whether it is high- or low-skilled work, younger or older workers, or male or female workers, the more relevant an individual's knowledge (explicit or tacit) is to today's employment needs, the more likely the individual is to be employed (and earn a higher income as well). **Table 3** presents recent stark data from the United States.

This relationship also holds for older individuals, the same people we want to encourage to continue sharing their productive capacity. In fact, more people continue to work into what was once thought to be old age. Economist and demographer Gary Burtless (2013) has written that equally important is "[t]he expectation that older workers will reduce average productivity . . . [which does] not necessarily describe the people who choose or who are permitted to remain in paid employment at older ages . . . there is little evidence that the aging workforce has hurt productivity" (p. 21).

Moreover, this human capital cohort is clearly not idle. **Figure 10** uses the United States to show workforce participation by age cohort.

Today's challenge is as much about how to maintain relevance in a workplace as it is about how to obtain knowledge. The pace of change itself seems to be faster than in the past: "As technology advances, the needs of the economy shift, and bad things happen if the skills of the labor force do not keep up," writes economist Bradford DeLong (2014).

---

[16]Author email exchange with Dr. Michael Roizen on 26 March 2015 to confirm (update) a prior citation from Mauldin (2013).

Table 3.   Earnings and Unemployment Rates by Educational Attainment

Highest Level Attained	Unemployment Rate in 2013	Median Weekly Earnings in 2013
Doctoral degree	2.2%	$1,623
Professional degree	2.3	1,714
Master's degree	3.4	1,329
Bachelor's degree	4.0	1,108
Associate's degree	5.4	777
Some college, no degree	7.0	727
High school diploma	7.5	651
Less than a high school diploma	11.0	472
All workers	6.1%	$827

Notes: Data are for persons age 25 and over. Earnings are for full-time wage and salary workers.
Sources: US Current Population Survey, US Bureau of Labor Statistics, and US Department of Labor.

Table 4 hints at the size of the problem. How can labor adjust to new technologies that seem to arrive both in greater number than ever before and also experience much faster adoption rates than in the past?

The *Economist* has reported:

> The industrial waves Kondratieff observed in the 1920s came every 50–60 years or so. By the late 1990s, fresh ones were arriving twice as often. Fifteen years on, their frequency appears to have doubled yet again. Waves of new innovations now seem to be rolling in every 10 to 15 years. ("Divining Reality from the Hype" 2014)

Regardless of whether you believe that future innovations will have limited further benefit or revolutionary potential,[17] innovation and re-combinations of past innovations will continue to affect employment opportunities. The most logical approach to dealing with these technological innovation waves is to update educational curricula faster than we have and create incentives for lifelong learning and the pursuit of continuous improvement.

For example, employers could make educational sabbaticals available to long-service workers. From a purely educational perspective, however, cautions Nobel Prize–winning economist Joseph Stiglitz (with coauthor Bruce Greenwald), "A reformed education system would take at least eight years before it could produce more highly trained graduates (because older classes

---

[17]An example of the debate between these points of view, exemplified by the economists Robert Gordon and Joel Mokyr, may be found in Aeppel (2014). For a perspective on this debate, see Siegel (2014).

Figure 10. Labor-Force Participation Growth Rate, 2000–July 2014

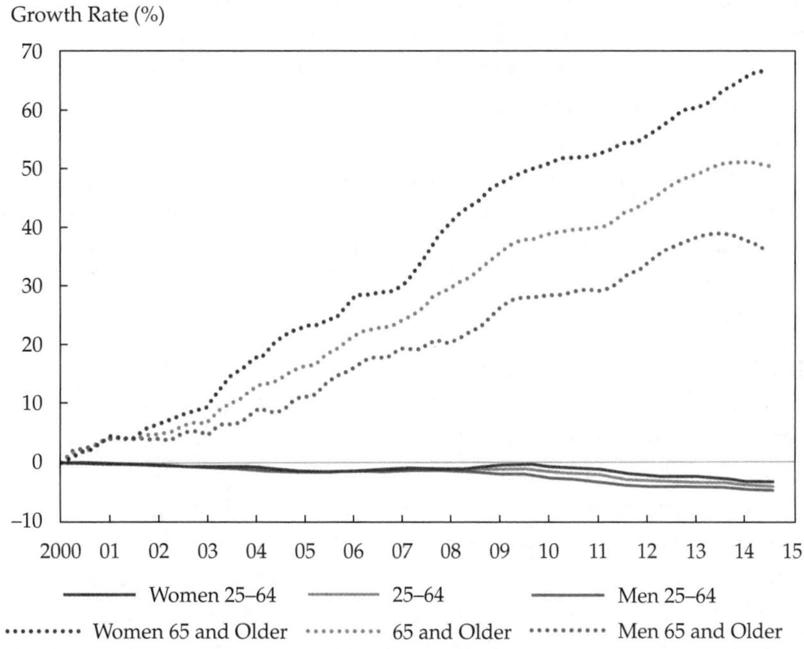

Growth Rate (%)

Women 25–64 ———— 25–64 ———— Men 25–64

·········· Women 65 and Older ·········· 65 and Older ·········· Men 65 and Older

Notes: Non-seasonally-adjusted 12-month moving average. In percentage terms, the growth rates by age/gender have been: 25–64, –4.0%; men 25–64, –4.6%; women 25–64, –3.2%; 65 and over, 50.3%; men 65 and over, 35.6%; women 65 and over, 67.1%.
Source: www.dshort.com (August 2014).

Table 4. Rate of Diffusion of New Technologies

Technology	Number of Years to Reach Half the US Population
Telephone	71
Electricity	52
Radio	28
Personal computer	19
Color TV	18
Cellphone	14
Internet access	10

Source: Thierer and Eskelsen (2008), p. 18.

would be inadequately prepared by their pre-reform training), and these graduates would transform the total labor force only slowly over time" (Stiglitz and Greenwald 2014, p. 33). But educational reform can never be enough, because learning continues far beyond one's formal school years. There are real shortcomings today in the efforts made toward continuous learning after college graduation. As jobs become more and more technical, the lack of ongoing learning becomes a primary contributor to employment challenges.

By the way, it is not just jobs that change and/or disappear over time. Employers also face the risk of extinction (Schumpeter's "creative destruction"[18]). Employers need to continuously build and replace their stock of human capital, to become lifelong-learning organizations.

Investment Capital. An important aspect is to differentiate, as Solow (1956) famously did, investment capital from savings. Savings can be used as investment capital, but they can also be used for consumption, negating their potential to contribute to productivity growth. So, what is the current state of investment capital (that could expand productive capacity)? Investment capital is well positioned to be used to enhance growth but is not without its own risks.

The owners and controllers of much of the world's investable capital—including societal-wide (sovereign) wealth funds, defined benefit (DB) pension trusts, and ultra-high-net-worth individuals—have either long-dated investment goals or no determinable time-frame needs for the return of their capital. Defined contribution (DC) plans—the fourth-largest capital controller—are directed by their participants and may have a shorter-term orientation than do DB trusts, but they have moved significantly toward target-date fund structures that are longer-term oriented and adjust investment allocations slowly. These four types of institutions direct the vast majority of the world's investable capital, and as one of Canada's premier institutional investors, Alberta Investment Management, has observed, they are advantaged by their long-term orientation: "Our Comparative Advantages Are Cash and Patience—We can earn a premium return for being able to commit sizeable capital for long periods of time. Unlisted investments must offer better returns than their closest listed proxy."[19] Unlisted investments include infrastructure and venture capital, which directly improve productive capacity, innovation, and economic growth.

Nevertheless, today this "patience" advantage faces (at least) three challenges that will eat away at productivity gains: interest rates, agedness, and trust issues.

---

[18]Harvard University economist Joseph A. Schumpeter (1883–1950).

[19]See Point 5 in the AIMCo investment philosophy at www.aimco.alberta.ca/How-We-Think/Investment-Philosophy.

■ *Interest rates.* Interest rates since the Great Recession of 2008 continue to be historically low, effectively zero for short-term bills and bonds, and may remain low for some time because of the deflationary impact of the "age wave" and the presence of a large amount of public debt almost everywhere in the world. Retired populations need income, and today's yields are woefully inadequate. So, retirees may consume more of their capital than they would if higher yields were available. Capital longevity is challenged.[20]

Structural impediments also affect long-term investing. Consider that, according to the Group of Thirty (an alliance of central bankers and economists):

> While U.S. bond, equity, and securitization markets are mature and liquid, this is not the case in much of the world. Banks are, and will remain for the medium term, the dominant source of external financing outside the United States, and commercial bank loan maturities average only 2.8 years in emerging economies and 4.2 years in developed economies—far shorter bond maturities. (G30 Working Group 2013, p. 14).

To further complicate long-term investing, numerous agency biases "pervade delegated investment management [and] are exacerbated when investing for the long term, where the payoff is distant and often highly uncertain. These conditions compound the difficulty of aligning and monitoring the agents (managers) responsible for making investment decisions, particularly across multi-layered investment organizations" (Neal and Warren 2015, p. 1).

Moreover, tax codes can either create an incentive for growth or retard long-term investments. For example, lower capital gains tax rates for longer-duration investments (e.g., at least five years) might reduce speculation, dampen market volatility, and potentially lower the risk of the stock market in the long run.

■ *Agedness.* The trend toward lower fertility rates and higher life expectancies will continue to increase dependency ratios, which are shown (and projected) for the developed and developing world in **Figure 11**. Labor participation rates are dropping, and retired populations, by definition, are consuming saved capital instead of investing it, further reducing potential productivity.

■ *Trust issues.* The general loss of trust in the financial services industry can be seen in the Edelman 2015 survey provided in **Table 5**. The loss of trust

---

[20]Some people, including apparently Janet Yellen, chair of the US Federal Reserve and chair of the Federal Open Market Committee, believe that low interest rates are more salutary than I've said. If the stimulating effect of low rates through the borrowing channel outweighs the wealth and income effects of low rates paid to savers, then even lower rates would improve the economic picture. Following Cochrane (2015) and Siegel and Coleman (2015), evidence is increasing that low rates are harmful to growth because of the low incomes (negative real incomes) paid to savers.

Figure 11. Old Age Dependency: Population Aged 65 and Over per 100 People Aged 25–64

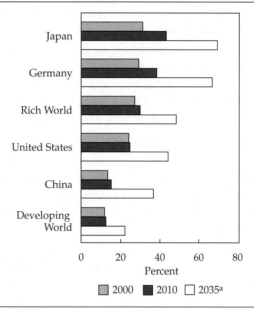

[a]Forecast.
Source: UN Population Division.

can positively affect short-term consumption at the cost of long-lived investment capital.

The developed countries already face (and the developing countries are not far behind) real challenges as to how productivity growth can and will help offset the loss of the demographic dividend—let alone bolster future economic growth (and support investments). In addition, the challenges discussed so far do not include those of a regulatory nature. Governing and taxing bodies need to be careful with their support for "what has been" versus "what could be" and be specifically supportive of innovation. A simple example is Google's pursuit of a driverless car; success would save lives and produce an extra 6 billion minutes of productive capacity per day in the United States alone (Urmson 2015). Technical success with the car is not, however, overall success; changes in laws will be needed, at a minimum. Innovation has been historically a net creator of jobs (Smith and Anderson 2014), but because of short-term job displacements, politicians often view innovation negatively.

The potential to increase productivity is *not* solely about pushing out the knowledge frontier, however, but also about technology diffusion. According to

Table 5. Trust in Institutions, 2015

Industries	Trust Score
Technology	78%
Consumer electronics	75
Automotive	71
Entertainment	67
Food and beverage	67
Consumer packaged goods	66
Brewing and spirits	63
Telecommunications	63
Pharmaceuticals	61
Energy	60
Consumer health	60
Chemicals	57
Financial services	54
Banks	53
Media	51

Source: 2015 Edelman Trust Barometer: www.edelman.com/insights/intellectual-property/ 2015-edelman-trust-barometer/trust-and-innovation-edelman-trust-barometer/executive-summary.

McKinsey Global Institute analysis, large populations around the world could benefit tremendously from the faster adoption of technologies that already exist. **Table 6** shows that for the G–19 countries, three-quarters of the productivity potential comes from "catch-up" growth and the rest from innovation. Businesses and policymakers need to think about how to speed this process.

It is time we address people and productivity policies—not only because we can, but when all is said and done, economic growth depends on it. Let's raise the quality of life for as many people as possible for as long as we can.

Table 6. Potential per Year Productivity Growth Rates

Global Category	Catching Up	Pushing the Frontier	Potential Growth Rate
G–19	75%	25%	4%
Developed	55	45	2
Emerging	82	18	6

Source: Manyika et al. (2015).

2. Entitlement to Responsibility with Appreciation (ERA)

> Don't go around saying the world owes you a living. The world owes you nothing. It was here first.
>
> — *Robert Jones Burdette (1844–1914)*

Did you learn to fish on your own or were you taught by someone else? Do you buy your fish at a market, or are fish simply given to you? Perhaps a little (expansive) perspective could help. Was it you and only you that succeeded at fishing? Even if you learned on your own, did you build or make your own fishing pole or dig up the bait used? In some manner or form, success almost always has some assistance, if only from Mother Nature or those who came before us. Can you appreciate the people, things, and circumstances that have enabled your success? Or do you, like so many, suffer from ADD—Appreciation Deficit Disorder? Are you "entitled"?

According to a Brookings Institution study, "About two-thirds of Americans (69 percent) agree with the statement that 'people are rewarded for intelligence and skill'; the highest percentage across 27 countries participating in an international survey of social attitudes conducted."[21]

How do you think those 69% think about entitlements (e.g., safety nets), responsibility, and appreciation? Surveys indicate that they have different beliefs compared with the remaining 31% about tax levels or the number of safety nets. And because taxes pay for entitlements, people who receive entitlements are perceived as not taking enough responsibility for their own success. Got "ADD"?

Figure 12 shows how US citizens, when compared with 27 other countries, believe skill more than luck drives success. Note that the United States is at the extreme high end of the belief that success is deserved. Perhaps it is no coincidence that the United States has "weaker" safety nets (relative to its wealth level) than most of the 27 countries surveyed. That's not a criticism but, rather, a clear indication that culture matters, where culture includes values, beliefs, and behavior.

In Chapter 1, I discussed the fact that the United States has attracted the majority of inventor emigrants in the world (because of meritocratic dreams?) whereas more noninventor emigrants have gone to Western

---

[21]Isaacs (2008). A number of more recent surveys support similar relative attitudes. In the United States, the "agree" scores for how people are rewarded have decreased to the 50% range.

Figure 12. Perceptions of Mobility and Inequality (2008)

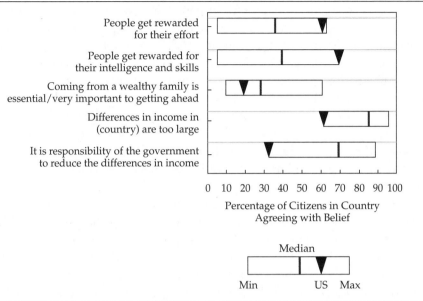

Source: Brookings Institution tabulation of data from the International Social Survey Programme, 1998–2001: www.issp.org.

Europe, possibly for their comparatively stronger safety nets. Yet, Western European attitudes toward immigration seem to be less positive than they are in the United States. Incentives matter: Does your culture encourage the practices and behaviors that are needed for economic growth, such as a welcoming attitude toward immigrants? Whether or not people actually calculate upside opportunity versus downside protection when making important decisions (such as where to live), they pursue what "feels" best, and doing so often serves them well.

The question is: What attitude is most likely to bolster productivity in an economy? It is responsibility. Unfortunately, that which feels best is not always a good bedfellow with responsibility.

Contrary to the views of Thomas Malthus (1798), who predicted that a growing population would starve, the past 200-plus years have witnessed both tremendous population growth and an increasing number of the people with "fish to eat," roofs over their heads, and positive outlooks. Even if we focus on only the more recent decades, life expectancy is up, infant mortality is down, and GDP per capita is up—globally. Human ingenuity has and continues to provide abundance; for more and more people around the world, life is good! Got appreciation or ADD?

Ironically, although Malthus's forecast of a huge increase in population was correct, that very growth in population was a key driver of the big boost in economic growth—the opposite of what he predicted. As shown in Chapter 1, however, for the developed world, demographics no longer work in our favor, and our focus must now turn to productivity to overcome the aging of the population. At the same time, too many people remain in poverty or at risk of poverty,[22] global economies are too indebted,[23] and entitlement policy reforms seem too far out of reach, if only as a result of populist sentiments and the orientation of most politicians. Entitlement to Responsibility with Appreciation has challenges, if only because of the potential reduction of safety-net comforts and new appreciation or respect needed for those in need of safety nets.

Although the bounty of human ingenuity is gratifying, we can and should strive to be better. We should pursue improvements in the *quality* of all lives (i.e., people's rights, freedom, independence) not just the *quantity* in some lives (i.e., material things). This pursuit could begin with a combination of greater requirements for personal responsibility and improved safety-net designs. Curiously, Lord Beveridge (William Beveridge, 1879–1963), who was dubbed the father of the welfare state in the United Kingdom in the early 1940s, wrote the following in 1948, "The State cannot see to the rendering of all the services that are needed to make a good society. One way of making this point would be to describe simply as Voluntary Services what is done by individual citizens, to supplement what is done as Social Service by the State" (p. 304).

Let's first acknowledge that growth in GDP is not, and has never been, a fully inclusive or accurate measure of economic progress; aspects of improved quality of life are difficult to capture in numerical terms. Simon Kuznets (1933), the Nobel Prize–winning economist who developed the system of national income accounting, said back in the 1930s, "The welfare of a nation can, therefore, scarcely be inferred from a measurement of national income" (p. 7). Economic growth and social progress are not identical.

For example, the costs of safety nets (or trampolines) are simply a transfer to those who no longer work or will never work again, but they could be, instead, an investment in those who can and are willing to work again. According to the business strategist Michael Porter, social progress is "the

---

[22]Poverty is best defined on a local scale rather than a global scale.

[23]Of course, there are real differences between debt that is private and debt that is public and between debt that is taken on for real investment (not margin borrowing but borrowing to buy real economic assets) and debt that is used for consumption. Bankruptcy laws can help ameliorate unmanageable private debt, but public (socialized) debt has fundamentally different challenges for monetary and fiscal systems. A survey of CFA charterholders in late 2015 reflects concern about public debt (see Hayat 2015).

capacity of a society to meet the basic human needs of its citizens, establish the building blocks that allow citizens and communities to enhance and sustain the quality of their lives, and create the conditions for all individuals to reach their full potential" (Porter, Stern, and Green 2014).

Figure 13 provides a grid that combines GDP with a measure of social progress.

That full potential is synonymous with maximizing the value of human capital and would certainly boost economic growth as it is pursued. We should also take note of the goal to "sustain the quality"; once the goal is reached, that is, it must be sustained. Improved safety-net designs can help sustain economic growth akin to what sustainable fishing could accomplish for the oceans and the environment.

A highly recommended initial step in the pursuit of full potential is for individuals to learn how to learn (more on this subject in Chapter 5). Once people learn how to learn, they have a skill that can enable them to

Figure 13.   Measuring Development: Social Progress Index and GDP per Person

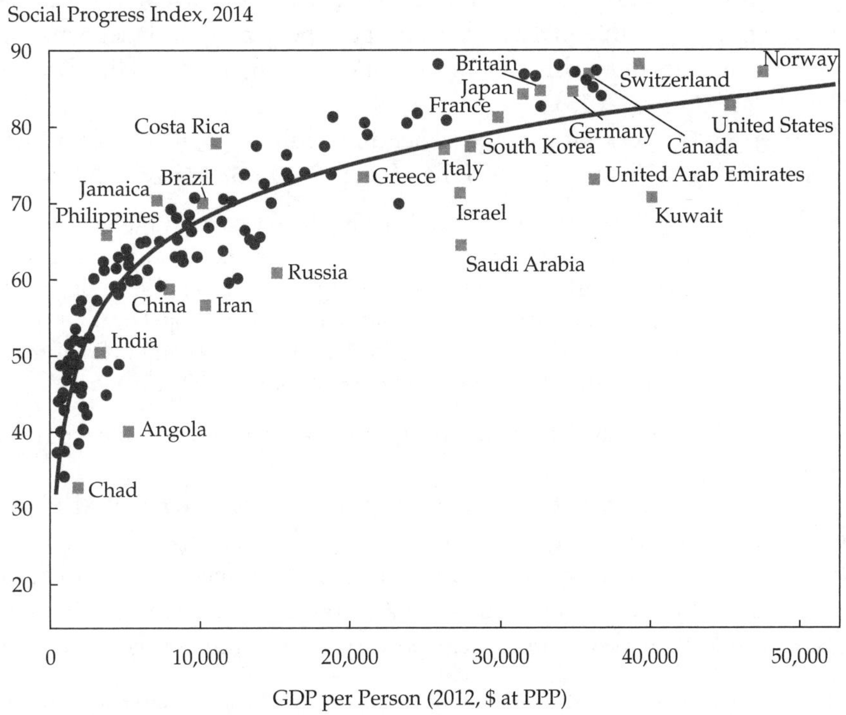

Note: PPP is purchasing power parity, 2005 prices.
Sources: Social Progress Imperative and Porter et al. (2014).

continuously improve (adapt) over time. Short of such a meta-technique, society can offer specific skills training, as in an adult jobs program.

Skills training should include all of the usual steps, such as from apprentice to journeyman, but should also include as much autonomy as early as possible. If we want to promote responsibility, then we must allow for failure as well as success. For individuals who are unable to take responsibility, there would be the safety nets. If more and more people can adopt the mindset that failure is nothing more than feedback—aided by the support of nets and trampolines—then growth toward our highest potential can become achievable. In fact, as Rajan and Zingales (2003) pointed out, nets encourage people to invest in their future. Of course, if success entails some risk, then the safety of a net makes the pursuit of success less risky and more likely. The opposite was clearly demonstrated when US bankruptcy laws were reformed in 2005 and the net was "removed." The result was a big jump in mortgage defaults and real costs to the financial industry (and the economy).

Moreover, not everyone is always able to take responsibility or bounce back from hardships. What if the public perception of those who need or use nets is wrong? Research by the World Bank "suggests that poverty constitutes a cognitive tax that makes it hard for poor people to think deliberatively, especially in times of hardship or stress... it's more than a shortfall of money" (World Bank Group 2015).

Poverty is one form of scarcity, as Sendhil Mullainathan and Eldar Shafir argue in their 2013 book *Scarcity: Why Having Too Little Means So Much*:

> This mindset [of scarcity] brings two benefits. It concentrates the mind on pressing needs. It also gives people a keener sense of the value of a dollar, minute, calorie, or smile . . . [But] this scarcity mindset can also be debilitating. It shortens a person's horizons and narrows his perspective, creating a dangerous tunnel vision. Anxiety also saps brainpower and willpower, reducing mental bandwidth. ("The Psychology of Scarcity" 2013).

Figure 14 illustrates how financial insecurity can consume cognitive resources.

Those of us who are not poor can sympathize: We too often make bad decisions in connection with our biology. When we are hungry, angry, lonely, or tired (HALT) or sick or injured, we tend to act foolishly.[24] These bad decisions are not irrational; they are suboptimal and, based on our biology, wholly human.[25] Please consider that people in or near poverty are not necessarily irresponsible

---

[24]Much research has been carried out into the neuroscience behind willpower and how present circumstances can influence our behavior and decisions. Among the published authors, see McGonigal (2013) and Baumeister and Tierney (2012).

[25]This topic was covered specifically by Falk (2011b).

Figure 14.   Financial Scarcity

Sugar cane farmers in Tamil Nadu, India, receive most of
their income once a year during the harvest. Immediately
before receiving their income (panel a), the same farmers
exhibit higher financial stress and lower cognitive scores,
relative to the postharvest period (panel b). This cannot
be explained by a change in nutrition, physical exhaustion,
biological stress, or a practice effect on the cognitive test.

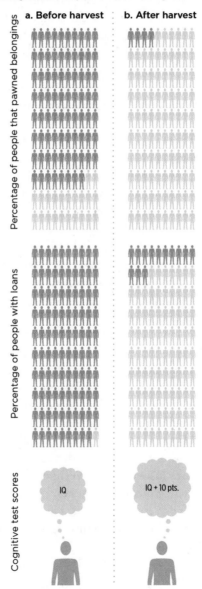

Source: Mani, Mullainathan, Shafir, and Zhao (2013).

or silly, lacking intelligence, or destined to live out their lives as Thomas Hobbes feared. People in or near poverty are more likely to make suboptimal decisions too often or at the worst possible times when their good decisions were otherwise "HALTed." Such decisions appear small but turn out to be costly.

Regardless of how well intentioned safety nets may be, however, they are incentives, and as incentives, they can and do produce behavior that is unwelcome. For example, drivers who wear seatbelts drive faster than those who do not, and this faster driving can negate the benefit of the seatbelt for themselves or (worse) for others (Peltzman 1975). Is it any surprise that older individuals may prefer to retire than to continue to work or that out-of-work individuals may not vigorously pursue employment because of the "comfort" a safety-net stipend offers? Nets that double as hammocks are not in the best interest of any economy.

The combination of aging populations, lower fertility rates, low labor participation rates, and strong populist sentiments has made present-day entitlements unsustainable. Ever-increasing use of entitlements in the developed world has costs that can only be afforded by higher taxes, which are a cost to economic growth (Romer and Romer 2007). Lower growth then, in turn, decreases taxable revenues, producing a vicious circle that is directly linked to entitlements. Beyond a certain level (and that level is so hard to determine), entitlements become economically dangerous. For now, it seems only the developed world has the immediate challenge to overcome.

Redistribution policies also pose a risk, albeit quite different from that of entitlements, to economic prosperity. Dutch economist Bas Jacobs argues that redistribution is costly and that social welfare declines, on average, with approximately 10 cents per euro that is redistributed.[26] Policies that tax wealthier individuals, those who can afford to pay more, may reduce their incentives to invest (or accurately report income) and may be an incentive to keep assets offshore. This effect may hurt productivity and, ultimately, the wages of those people most in need of employment or assistance.

It is not that the wealthier among us should not pay more. It is that we simply do not know at what level high tax rates become economically destructive. When US Supreme Court Justice Oliver Wendell Holmes (1841–1935) said, "Taxes are the price of civilized society,"[27] he was correct, but he never said how much civilization should cost. Reasonable people can argue for vastly different tax rates. A century after Holmes, economist Arthur Laffer showed that there

---

[26]See www.eur.nl/ese/english/news/detail/article/76042-bas-jacobs-book-price-of-equality-presented-to-state-secretary-for-finance-eric-wiebe.

[27]In *Compañía General de Tabacos de Filipinas* v. *Collector of Internal Revenue*, 275 U.S. 87, 100 (1927).

is a single tax rate, somewhere between 0% and 100%, that maximizes government revenue.[28] Similarly, there is a tax rate that maximizes civilization (given some definition of it). These rates may be the same or different, and debates about how to resolve these questions are the central political problem of our time. Moreover, attempts to discover the rates may put economic growth at risk, especially considering the power of those with special pleadings to increase a rate and the relative impotence of those who pay it.

Nevertheless, a tax rate that helps maximize an economy's productive capacity is desirable. Without economic growth, funding entitlements will become an enormous, if not intractable, handicap for all economies. So, the choice to pursue economic growth is simple.

The execution, however, is not easy. Future growth is far less certain than the cost of the promises we make today (the future liabilities). Except in the few countries that have youthful populations today, or where significant entitlement promises have not (yet) been made, policymakers need to take heed of the admonition "when you find yourself in a hole, stop digging."[29] Furthermore, youthful populations have their own growth challenges. For example, the average Chinese citizen saves more than others globally in part because safety nets are not available (Yang, Zhang, and Zhou 2011), and that high savings rate is widely thought to potentially restrain future Chinese growth.

Safety nets can be a problem whether they are strong or weak. For this reason, solely cutting benefits is not the answer to lagging economic growth, and updated policy designs are necessary; these designs must require *responsibility* along with providing nets and trampolines. For example, **Exhibit 2** provides an idea as to how safety and responsibility could be combined in an improved type of unemployment insurance system (payments to unemployed workers until they find new work). In the "best concept," the overall cost of the insurance would drop and the unemployed person would have an increased responsibility to find/start any work, but over the full 12 months of the current unemployment safety net, more money could be earned than with benefits alone.

Some argue that the weaknesses of the safety-net system prove the need for more "civic capital," defined by Guiso, Sapienza, and Zingales (2010) as "those persistent and shared beliefs and values that help a group overcome the free-rider problem in the pursuit of socially valuable activities" (p. 3). Is this not the concept of a social contract we are looking for? Should those who have made the transition from unemployment to employment not be rewarded?

---

[28]The Laffer curve is named after Arthur Laffer, an economist who was part of President Ronald Reagan's Economic Policy Advisory Board. The curve is alleged to have been initially drawn on a napkin.

[29]Sometimes attributed to Will Rogers (1879–1935).

Exhibit 2.   Unemployment Concept

Current Unemployment Safety Net (example)	Better Safety Net	Best Concept: Trampoline to 12 Months
≤12 months of stipends; ends when any employment income is reported	≤6 months of stipends, but a trampoline can extend stipends for up to 12 months	Beginning Month 7: The stipend can continue if there is verifiable income, but the two together must be ≤150% of the stipend, and the stipend cannot increase. At Month 13, all stipends = 0.

Note: This chart summarizes the author's policy concept and does not reflect empirical findings or the outputs of a formal model.

The French economist Thomas Piketty (2014) addressed the obvious reality that wealth inequality exists and has grown (within some countries) over time. But would it not have been more helpful if he had explored the underlying *causes* of wealth inequality?[30] Yes, income inequality exists, but why? And what can be constructively done about it? After all, if the "winners" could not win, why would they play?

One US researcher, Diana Furchtgott-Roth of the Manhattan Institute for Policy Research, even calls into question Piketty's conclusion that income inequality is expanding: "Much of this concern is a problem in search of reality caused by problems of measurement and changes in demographic patterns over the past quarter-century. Government data on spending patterns show remarkable stability over the past 25 years and, if anything, a narrowing rather than an expansion of inequality" (2013). Note that she is focusing not on market income but on consumption, which includes social transfers—safety-net stipends. Regardless, recessions happen, and savings used to help make ends meet will no longer be available to grow when growth returns. Job losses among those with lower incomes and less savings materially contribute to wealth inequality. It is not maniacal; it is math.

If we are to be seriously concerned with inequality, it should be *opportunity inequality*, not income or wealth inequality. The drivers of opportunity are human capital and productivity, which are inputs or independent variables, in contrast to outputs or dependent variables, such as income and wealth. If we fail to deal with the causes of wealth inequality and try simply to adjust the

---

[30]I would also note that the recent period identified by Piketty as having the greatest increase in inequality within developed countries, roughly 1970–2012, had the greatest *decrease* in between-countries inequality. China, India, and other developing countries were significantly catching up with the developed world.

outcomes to achieve some desired result, more "have-nots" will want more safety nets and stoke the fire of populism.

Neither more taxation nor redistribution helps economic growth, and each is more likely to restrain it and to expand inequality. Skillful redesigns of the system to reduce unintended negative consequences are one of the keys to bolstering economic growth, which we know will reduce the problem. Such a redesign is not easy—if it were, we would have already done it—but it is worth the work needed to figure out how to do it. Consider the following from Warren Buffett (1998):

> Let's just say, Sandy, that it was 24 hours before you were born, and a genie appeared, and said "Sandy, you look like a winner. I have enormous confidence in you, and what I'm going to do is let you set the rules of the society into which you will be born. You can set the economic rules, the social rules, and whatever rules you set will apply during your lifetime, and your children's lifetimes."
>
> And you'll say, "Well that's nice, but what's the catch?"
>
> And the genie says, "Here's the catch. You don't know if you're going to be born rich or poor, white or black, male or female, able-bodied or infirm, intelligent or retarded. All you know is that you're going to get one ball [out] of a barrel with, say, 5.8 billion balls in it. You're going to participate in what I call the Ovarian Lottery. And it's the most important thing that will happen to you in your life, but you have no control over it. It's going to determine far more than your grades at school or anything else that happens to you.
>
> "Now, what rules do you want to have? I'm not going to tell you the rules, and nobody will tell you; you have to make them up for yourself. But, they will affect how you think about what you do in your will and things of that sort. That's because you're going to want to have a system that turns our great quantities of good[s] and services, so that your kids can live better than you did, and so that your grandchildren can live better than your kids. You're going to want a system that keeps Bill Gates and Andy Grove and Jack Welch working long, long after they don't need to work. You're going to want the most able people working for more than 12 hours a day. So you've got to have a system that [incents] them, and that turns out goods.
>
> "But you're also going to want a system that takes care of the bad balls, the ones that aren't lucky. If you have a system that is turning out enough goods and services, you can take care of them. You want a system where people are free of fear to some extent. You don't want people worrying about being sick in their old age, or fearful about going home at night. So you'll try to design something, assuming you have the goods and services to solve that sort of thing. You'll want equality of opportunity—a good school system—to

make you feel that every piece of talent out there will get the same shot at contributing. And your tax system will follow from your reasoning on that. And what you do with your money you make is another thing to think about. As you work through that, everybody comes up with something a little different. I just suggest you play that little game." (p. 12)

Now, that is a reframe of income inequality! Interestingly, although academics seem to argue endlessly, they generally agree on the three key factors that contribute to opportunity. They are: (1) stable household environments, (2) good schools, and (3) good early-childhood nutrition. I will cover each of these in some detail.

Unfortunately, some of these factors have an actual time limit—for example, types of childhood nutrition that drive specific development. The benefits of good childhood nutrition must be experienced by a certain age to be meaningful at all. In the transcript, Buffett posed his questions to Sandy prior to her birth, and although prebirth factors (which do exist and are important) are beyond the scope of this book, those that arise at birth are not. Opportunity equality is primarily a childhood issue (Allen and Kelly 2015). Our goal should be to support these three key factors to the extent possible (access to schools and nutrition will be addressed in Chapter 5):

1. Stable household environments. This factor positively affects a range of other factors. First and foremost, unstable households experience increased stress, which can damage brain development in children (World Bank Group 2015). Beyond the biological effects, the kind of unremitting stress that takes place in highly unstable households is conducive to unproductive, dangerous, and even destructive behavior. **Figure 15** shows the effect of stress on the brain.

   Unstable households also face a higher risk of poverty. Poverty, in turn, negatively affects where one lives, impairs access to quality schools, and increases the possibility of hunger.

2. Access to good public schools. The lifelong building blocks of reading, writing, mathematics, and early socialization skills are critically important, but not all children have equal access to schools that provide these skills (Annie E. Casey Foundation 2014). Quality education is not universally available, and where one lives and how much income one earns does, sadly, matter. As documented by the Annie E. Casey Foundation, gaps exist in fourth-grade reading proficiency scores in the United States between low-income and high-income students. These gaps, however, are not fully descriptive of the potential for improvement. Gaps can be closed

Figure 15.   Unrelenting Stress

Toxic stress is the strong, unrelieved activation of the body's stress management system. This image depicts neurons in the brain areas most important for successful learning and behavior—the hippocampus and prefrontal cortex. The neuron shown in panel b, which has been subjected to toxic stress, clearly displays underdeveloped neural connections.

a. Typical neuron: many connections

b. Neuron damaged by toxic stress: fewer connections

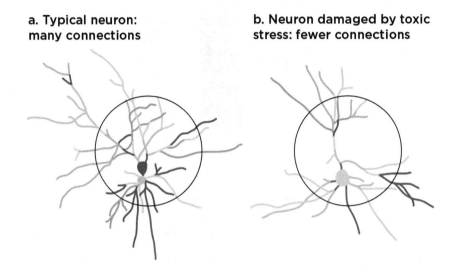

Source: Shonkoff et al. (2012).

with proper interventions. This same principle applies in many different countries. As an example, **Figure 16** shows the data for villages in India and how a caste can affect classroom performance.

3.   Access to nutrition in the early years of childhood. This access is critical because those years are the most significant in terms of brain development. Irreparable harm can be done without proper nutrition in that period. Beyond the concerns about nutrition, too many children simply experience hunger. **Figure 17** provides statistics on the effects of malnutrition globally.[31]

Parental or societal responsibility, safety nets, and trampolines can function in combination to create equal opportunities. The economy will benefit over the long term as more and more people prosper and thrive. Expenditures on these desirables do not represent costs solely; they are (or should be) investments in our collective future. After all, healthy and educated children

---

[31]See http://thousanddays.org/the-issue/acute-malnutrition.

Figure 16. Effects of Cuing a Stigmatized or Entitled Identity

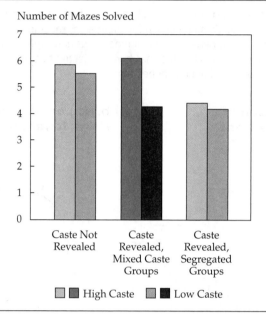

Number of Mazes Solved

Notes: High-caste and low-caste boys from villages in India were randomly assigned to groups that varied the salience of caste identity. When their caste was not revealed, high-caste and low-caste boys were statistically indistinguishable in solving mazes. Revealing caste in mixed classrooms decreased the performance of low-caste boys. However, publicly revealing caste in caste-segregated classrooms—a marker of high-caste entitlement—depressed the performance of both high-caste and low-caste boys. Again, their performance was statistically indistinguishable.
Source: Hoff and Pandey (2006).

are much more likely to contribute to instead of detracting from productivity growth as adults.

It is time for a new ERA, one in which taxation (perspectives on tax principles can be found in **Appendix 1**) is thought of as the building of civic capital based on the alignment of incentives with the needed degree of responsibility and the appropriate measure of appreciation.

As Part I closes and we turn to some solutions for the problems, please consider the following thoughts.

We have normality. I repeat, we have normality. Anything you still can't cope with is therefore your own problem.

—*Douglas Adams*

Figure 17.   Malnutrition

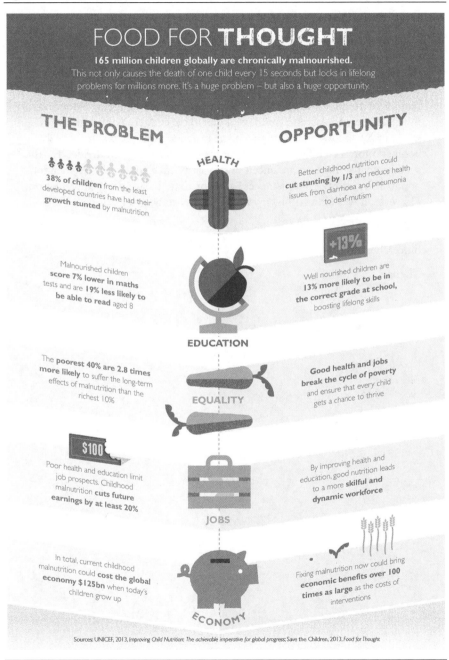

FOOD FOR **THOUGHT**

165 million children globally are chronically malnourished.
This not only causes the death of one child every 15 seconds but locks in lifelong problems for millions more. It's a huge problem – but also a huge opportunity.

THE PROBLEM

OPPORTUNITY

HEALTH

38% of children from the least developed countries have had their growth stunted by malnutrition

Better childhood nutrition could **cut stunting by 1/3** and reduce health issues, from diarrhoea and pneumonia to deaf-mutism

Malnourished children **score 7% lower in maths** tests and are **19% less likely to be able to read** aged 8

+13%

Well nourished children are **13% more likely to be in the correct grade at school,** boosting lifelong skills

EDUCATION

The **poorest 40% are 2.8 times more likely** to suffer the long-term effects of malnutrition than the richest 10%

EQUALITY

Good health and jobs break the cycle of poverty and ensure that every child gets a chance to thrive

$100

Poor health and education limit job prospects. Childhood malnutrition **cuts future earnings by at least 20%**

By improving health and education, good nutrition leads to a more **skilful and dynamic workforce**

JOBS

In total, current childhood malnutrition could **cost the global economy $125bn** when today's children grow up

Fixing malnutrition now could bring **economic benefits over 100 times as large** as the costs of interventions

ECONOMY

Sources: UNICEF, 2013, *Improving Child Nutrition: The achievable imperative for global progress*; Save the Children, 2013, *Food for Thought*

Source: Save the Children.

Do you appreciate your responsibility?

Dear Mr. Burdette:

Regarding your quote, which opened this chapter ("Don't go around saying the world owes you a living. The world owes you nothing. It was here first."), the world owes this author nothing. I was born a Caucasian male in the United States, grew up in a stable household, lived in a good neighborhood, had access to quality schools, and never experienced hunger. Furthermore, my childhood/adolescence witnessed global peace (generally), and my generation (X) followed one of the biggest generations in history (the baby boomers) for the "bifecta" of both peace and demographic dividends. The success that I have experienced was vastly enabled by the tremendous opportunity of my circumstances, and for that, I have great appreciation. However, it was (and still is) my responsibility to be productive.

Thank you.

Sincerely,

Michael

Part II: What Could (Should) Be the Next ERA?

Each chapter in this part closes with a "to-do" list for the subject that you can and should consider doing today. In Part II, I will explore how updated retirement, health care, and education policies might put us on a better and more sustainable path to growth.

3.   Let's Retire Retirement (as we know it)

Work saves us from three great evils: boredom, vice, and need.

—*Voltaire (1694–1778)*, Candide, *1759*

I agree with Voltaire. In addition, retirement is risky to a person's health, reduces the stock of valuable human capital, deprives many employers of a valuable resource, and negatively affects overall economic productivity. Given the exorbitant costs of retirement borne by individuals—Voltaire's "evils"— and given society's needs, why did retirement become policy and why is there the continued and intense interest in retiring?

Of course, some individuals will become no longer able to work, some will wish to pursue something new (human capital creation), and some will simply choose leisure. But none of these three groups requires any outside incentive(s) to stop working. Many, however—I fear, too many—dislike their jobs and work simply because they need to; they cannot think [dream?] of anything other than retiring.

So, how did retirement as public policy ever get started? The historical record indicates that German Chancellor Otto von Bismarck instituted a public retirement income guarantee in 1889 to defend against the threat of Marxism. Of course, factory and farm work were much more difficult and dangerous in Bismarck's time than they have been for many decades. Decades later, in the United States, President Franklin Roosevelt proposed Social Security following both a successful voluntary railroad retirement program in the 1920s and the Great Depression, which resulted in significant job loss. Keep in mind that 65 was "strategically" chosen by Bismarck (after choosing 70 and modifying it to 65 for greater acceptance) as an age that the majority of individuals would not attain. Neither historical event fits the reasons individuals seek to retire today.

If we wanted to view this history with rose-colored glasses, then individuals who were no longer able or less capable to work (referred to as "olders" in agrarian and industrial economies in the late 19th and early 20th centuries) stepped aside in favor of those who were younger and more capable. Here is how yesteryear's flowers became today's weeds.

First, the retirement policy was an honest appreciation of the fact that older individuals' labor capabilities had eroded. Given the era when retirement was "born," that is perfectly reasonable. Today, older individuals have never had more productive potential. Time will tell whether today's olders will embrace working longer to complement their increased longevity. Their productive abilities are needed by society today to counter negative demographic effects. Thus, retirement policies need to evolve to bolster economic growth. A more "compassionate" and productive policy could allow for varied retirement ages based on worker capabilities; such a policy is described in **Exhibit 3**. The gaming of the proposed approach would be highly unlikely. For example, people employed as consultants are unlikely to switch in their later years to construction work. The approach also contains a subtle beneficial incentive to file one's taxes.

The goal is to expand worker participation, enhance productivity, and match increased life expectancy with increased years of work. Underlying this concept is the idea that individuals could have multiple careers during their lifetime, with their skills, abilities, and health evolving to match the needs of those careers.

A major consideration in Exhibit 3 is the sustainability of retirement income in an era of ever greater longevity. As people age, they need to transition to work with fewer physical demands. With the extension of work spans, the need for retirement benefits and savings is reduced while social safety-net revenues expand. Regardless of these effects, savings for retirement should

Exhibit 3. Compassionate, Productive Retirement Policy

Current Retirement Policy (example)	A Better, Compassionate, Productive Retirement Policy (example)
Upon reaching age 65, you are officially retired and may begin to receive your social security/first pillar benefits[a]	In the past 10 years, have you been employed for at least 7 of those years in any of the following types of physical work (e.g., construction, in which dynamic or trunk strength, kneeling, bending, or crouching in difficult working conditions) is necessary? Please note that your response will be verified with your tax filings, and falsification will be penalized.
	▪ If yes, then you may retire at age 65 and begin to receive benefits.
	▪ If no, or if you have no tax filing evidence to support your claim, then you cannot retire until age 70 and may begin to receive benefits at that time.

Older individuals have productive capacity, but it is not "career balanced." Consider these points:
• Continued work with little productive capacity is of little societal value.
• The approach described in Exhibit 3 helps to balance life expectancy with retirement. Current policy favors the long-lived over laborers. Note that this example uses common retirement ages, not longevity or dependency-ratio-adjusted ages, which today would equate age 65 to roughly ages 72–73 in developed economies.
• Knowledge workers, who are able to work longer, could provide increased societal value.
• Workers with physically demanding work who transitioned to less demanding work earlier may preserve retirement at age 65 if they pass a "12 out of the past 20 years" test versus the "7 out of the past 10 years" test.

[a]"First pillar" refers to a standardized term for government/state-run basic pension benefits.

always be encouraged. Ideally, for the able-bodied and able-minded, *part-time* retirement should be financially encouraged—not only to meet society's needs but also to improve the aging individual's own self-esteem and health.

More than compassion is needed to determine appropriate retirement ages. The economists and demographers Skirbekk, Loichinger, and Weber (2012) write,

> Comparing the burden of aging across countries hinges on the availability of valid and comparable indicators. The Old Age Dependency Ratio allows only a limited assessment of the challenges of aging, because it does not include information on any individual characteristics except age itself. Existing alternative indicators based on health or economic activity suffer from measurement and comparability problems. We propose an indicator based on age variation in cognitive functioning. We use newly released data from standardized tests of seniors' cognitive abilities for countries from different world regions. In the wake of long-term advances in countries' industrial composition, and technological advances, the ability to handle new job procedures is now of high and growing importance, which increases the importance of cognition for work performance over time. In several countries with older populations, we find better cognitive performance on the part of populations aged 50+ than in countries with chronologically younger populations. (p. 1)

Moreover, they continue,

> This variation in cognitive functioning levels may be explained by the fact that seniors in some regions of the world experienced better conditions during childhood and adult life, including nutrition, duration and quality of schooling, lower exposure to disease, and physical and social activity patterns. (p. 1)

It is not solely age that matters; the level at which opportunity is made equal clearly matters.

Second, when retirement was established as social policy, the younger age cohort was short of employment opportunities and in need of help. At that time, the supply of jobs may have seemed to have been somewhat fixed, whereas today, the supply of jobs is clearly not fixed. Yet, evidence today, as shown in **Figure 18,** demonstrates that the older generations have remained in the workforce to the detriment of younger generations. Note how the Great Recession (shaded area) negatively affected the younger age cohorts more than the older age cohorts. Older individuals who continue to work can be a huge economic positive but only to the extent that total employment grows—which is neither guaranteed nor evidenced.

Figure 18 shows only US data, but a similar "crowding-out" of younger by older workers exists in other countries. When younger workers are unable to find work, household formation is reduced (they tend to move back in with

Figure 18. US Growth Rate in Labor Force Participation, 2000–2015

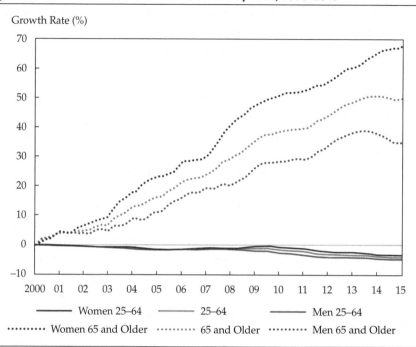

Note: Data are through January.

Source: www.advisorperspectives.com/dshort/updates/demographic-trends-in-employment-partici-pation (February 2015).

their parents) as is family formation, which hurts economic growth in the long run. The question remains as to how this recent trend may play out.

Jobs may not be static, but they also do not grow commensurately with the population in a lockstep fashion. The disconnect worsens in recessionary periods (e.g., 2008) and is made worse by an educational system that does not, or cannot, change its curriculum quickly enough to adjust to short-term job market trends. Job market flexibility is also impaired when labor laws impose high fixed costs (for example, medical benefits or required job security) on hiring so that companies would rather hire two or more part-time workers than one full-time worker.[32]

[32]In the United States, as of this publication date, because of the Affordable Care Act, employers with at least 50 full-time employees have to offer health insurance or pay a penalty. The incentive is to reduce full-time employment or limit worker hours to 30 (not full-time status) in order to avoid the medical insurance coverage requirement if possible. This rule reverses the preference for one full-time employee over more than one part-time employee. It exacerbates the growing number of part-timer workers, who might otherwise be hired full time. The concept of "making it up" with more than one part-time job is fallacious; maintaining schedules across multiple employers is far from a given possibility.

Educational systems are not completely responsible for this misalignment. The output of educational institutions can and does understandably become misaligned with short-term job opportunities for reasons embedded in what agricultural economists call "cobweb theory." Farmers, like everyone else, rely on price signals to determine how much of a good to produce. Raising a pig takes a long time, however, so the following sequence of events happens: (1) a farmer observes a high price in the market for pigs; (2) he decides to increase supply by raising more pigs; (2) by the time the pig is grown, the price has fallen because all other farmers have responded to the same signal and raised their own pigs; and so on, in a never-ending boom-and-bust cycle. We never get quite the right number of pigs. This observation is called cobweb theory because of the appearance of a graph of the price and quantity of pigs over time. It is the same with education: An increase in the demand for engineers in year zero will produce a surplus of engineers in year four, which will produce a shortage in year eight, and so on. Supply and demand are always imbalanced. (Education will be covered more specifically in Chapter 5.)

Economists Stephen Cecchetti and Enisse Kharroubi (2015) examined the growth effects of a specific supply–demand imbalance, the one we are currently experiencing in financial services: "First, the growth of a country's financial system is a drag on productivity growth. That is, higher growth in the financial sector reduces real growth. In other words, financial booms are not, in general, growth-enhancing, likely because the financial sector competes with the rest of the economy for resources" (p. 25).

Conceptually, younger generations could more easily become educated or trained for newer or more technical jobs than older workers—if only because of their greater risk capacity (they have few, if any, obligations) and the low opportunity cost of their time at this stage of their lives. That risk capacity also aligns nicely with where the greater preponderance of job growth tends to come from: "New and young companies are the primary source of job creation in the American economy. Not only that, but these firms also contribute to economic dynamism by injecting competition into markets and spurring innovation" (Wiens and Jackson 2015, p. 1). Increased total employment depends on a combination of the right skill(s) and the will or proper incentive(s) to work.

So, late 19th- and early 20th-century politics started the hole in which we are still digging. Stop digging! Put your shovels down! Let's review some key points:

- If people do not live beyond age 65, on average, then retirement at that age as a social goal and policy poses little harm. But today, longevity in the developed world has far surpassed age 65, and it continues to improve.

This trend poses ever greater risk of harm to the economies that do not acknowledge the need to update retirement age(s).

- When the working population is many times larger than the retiree population, retirement works, but this type of demography no longer describes developed economies. It is also unlikely to remain descriptive of developing economies in the near future because of their own positive gains in longevity and negative fertility trends. Consider that even China recently (October 2015) abandoned its long-held one-child policy out of fear of a declining population and worker shortages. Nevertheless, given the shape of China's population pyramid and its shortage of female births relative to male births, this change may be too late.

- If productivity levels are such that enough goods and services are available for all, retirement may be workable. Although this situation, which was a dream of John Maynard Keynes (1930), might be in the realm of possibility, current trends in population and productivity make it something to be contemplated only for the far future—if ever. Considering the world as a whole, the availability of goods and services for all has arguably never been possible and is highly unlikely in the foreseeable future. (Classical economics posits that needs and wants can never be satiated.) This observation highlights the key importance of enhancing world productivity. Might robots, ironically, be recast as the saviors of our future retirements versus the job stealers of today?

To what extent, if any, should retirement [at age 65? at any age?] remain a societal policy or goal? If we aspire to have great societies, then we need to offer safety nets. Not every older individual is capable of working. And many others, although able to work a little, may not be productive or well paid, so their lifetime savings may not be enough to sustain them in retirement. Society will always contain those who have a shortfall. As previously noted, the nets must not become hammocks, however, for older individuals who can work but choose not to. If we want to maintain the rate of productivity growth (short of any productivity miracles) to provide sustainable retirement policies, we will need to differentiate individual capabilities, maximize personal responsibility and opportunity, and offer a proper safety net for those who are not able to work and cannot sustain themselves.

First Principles for a Retirement Policy

This section provides a framework for a sustainable retirement policy but not a complete policy.

#1. Differentiation by Individual Capabilities. First and foremost, policies must be sustainable over long periods of time. This plan begins with a "sovereign retirement age" (the earliest age of eligibility) that itself will age and adjust over time (e.g., every 10 years) to fit a society's demography and preserve its productive capacity. As shown in the compassionate retirement example in Exhibit 3, the plan should have two retirement ages. Having only one retirement age forgoes the opportunity to increase work span substantially. Having more than two ages breeds complexity and potential gaming.

The goal is to base benefit payments on expected mortality as it relates to an individual's work, rather than basing payments on chronological age. According to a study by Rho (2010), "45% of workers who are 58 or older have a physically demanding job or work in difficult working conditions" (see Table 1, p. 5). It is not difficult to understand how working to an older age is far less possible for these workers than for those with less physically demanding work. Perhaps not surprisingly, there is a general correlation between income and being spared performing physically demanding jobs. The higher the income of workers and employees, the less likely they are to have physically demanding jobs.

Additional considerations include the following:

- Career gaming—that is, claiming inaccurately to be in a physically demanding job—will be highly unlikely if tax returns are required to demonstrate that, for example, 7 of the 10 years prior to retirement were spent in a particular career. Would individuals alter their career choice(s) to enable an earlier retirement? If so, that's fine; such an incentive system might foment a jobs rotation from more sophisticated work toward simpler work, which, in turn, would open up more career-oriented jobs for younger generations. Still, changing careers to accelerate retirement benefits is likely to be an uncommon choice.

- Individuals should always be free—as they are now—to retire earlier than the age at which benefits begin to be paid. Such early retirement would be "on their own dime" and nobody else's. The right to retire early and collect benefits is presently a massive challenge for many private and public pension systems. It is important to agree that no retirement payment would be issued until a person reached retirement age. The single exception could be for a verifiable and qualified disability (to be reviewed annually). Because of the high cost of retirement, retiring early would not likely be prevalent or pose productivity risks to an economy.

If retirement policy in your country is not sustainable, think hard about whether to maintain existing retirement incentives. As an alternative to changing the retirement age, you could pursue policies to bolster your work-force: welcome immigrants (would they want to immigrate to your country?), encourage women to join the workforce (as is being done, slowly, in Japan[33]), and/or aggressively leverage robots to satisfy your country's productivity needs.

#2. Strong Safety Net. A strong safety net would be put in place to support the two retirement ages. The most sustainable safety net is a "sovereign-sized" (country-wide) DB plan. Such a plan provides a monthly annuity stipend for as long as an individual is alive. Annuities work by pooling individuals so that longer-lived individuals receive a subsidy ("mortality credits") from those who drop out of the pool by dying. These credits are often estimated to increase the annuity stipend amounts by 20% or more.[34] Of course, an annuity is only as good as the credit of its issuer. The bigger and more diverse the pool of individuals, the smaller the risk of default as a result of adverse selection (which would occur if only those expecting a long life joined the annuity pool). Other sources of risk to the annuitant remain, however, such as risky investing by the issuer. Smaller or less diverse pools are not as sustainable, so private and public pension plans are riskier than sovereign-scaled plans but not nearly as risky as individually managed retirement portfolios. Following are some additional safety-net perspectives:

- This net should have just one insurance purpose—to provide monthly income to retired individuals. If additional insurance features are desired (i.e., unemployment or disability benefits), they should be priced separately to be standalone and self-supportive programs. Disability protection, for example, makes sense because it is expensive and not generally available to all individuals. Although mortality continues to improve, morbidity (lack of wellness) has also risen, increasing the cost of providing disability benefits.

- As insurance, the net would be only for those in need; monthly stipends should be means tested. But, no means tests would take place until all of the individual's past personal safety-net (tax) payments had been refunded[35] through the monthly stipends, dollar on dollar with no interest.[36] Only at this point would the means test occur. The result would reduce one's stipend in increments of 25%, potentially down to zero.

---

[33]See Matsui, Suzuki, Tatebe, and Akiba (2014).

[34]Waring and Siegel (2007) calculated a much larger number, 35%.

[35]In the United States, the math is interesting: The average individual receives a 100% refund of his or her lifetime Social Security taxes, dollar on dollar, within 60 months.

[36]To protect against sovereign profligacy, these repayments could include interest if/when inflation exceeds some chosen rate, such as 5%.

Those who lost their entire stipend would regain it once they reached the age of their expected mortality (say, age 83), and the stipend would adjust upward (downward) for inflation (deflation) for the balance of their lives.

Monthly stipend reductions would be based on the individual's preretirement reported income as averaged over the prior decade and compared with local poverty thresholds. For example, a nonstipend income of 12 times the poverty level could mean a 100% reduction in the stipend, whereas a nonstipend income of 3 times the poverty level could mean a 25% reduction. Failure to credibly report income during that prior decade could be penalized with an automatic, additional 50% reduction. Could such a requirement motivate more honest income reporting?

Such a system increases the personal responsibility of high-income individuals to save, but the responsibility is fitting because these individuals have the income to do so. In addition, high-income individuals tend to live the longest and are thus the most expensive for annuity issuers. **Figure 19** shows the Preston curve relating life expectancy to wealth for the world in 2006.[37]

---

[37]The Preston curve depicts an empirical cross-sectional relationship between life expectancy and real per capita income. It is named after Samuel H. Preston, who first described it in 1975.

Figure 19. Preston Curve, 2006

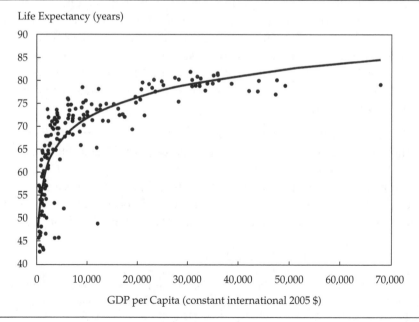

Note: Life expectancy = 6.6354(ln GDP per capita) + 10.754.

Table 7 provides the change in life expectancy from age 55 for men and women in the United States by income as concluded by Barry Bosworth of the Brookings Institution and reported in the *Wall Street Journal*.

Keep in mind that the lowered cost of this program would allow for decreased taxation and offer more discretionary savings potential (i.e., de facto privatization of a sovereign retirement system) for high-income individuals.

- The net would be funded through taxation. With both an increase in the retirement age and means testing of benefits, the net's sustainability should materially improve. The resulting lower liabilities could allow for lower taxation, a cap on taxable income, or perhaps an increase in benefits (a stronger net) to help replace the less sustainable private and nonsovereign public pension plans.

- Because this safety net should be funded (become funded over time), how the "account" would be invested by a government is no small matter. Of primary concern are the potential conflicts of interest that arise when government officials are in charge of investment decisions. Specifically, allowable investments and their allocations should be set—for example, short-term government bonds (for liquidity needs less than three years), local inflation-linked bonds with maturities greater than three years (which could help manage local government profligacy or even help

Table 7. Change from Age 55 in Life Expectancy by Income

	Change for US Men	Change for US Women
Richest 10%	5.9	3.1
81%–90%	5.3	2.4
71%–80%	4.9	1.8
61%–70%	4.6	1.4
51%–60%	4.2	1.0
41%–50%	3.9	0.5
31%–40%	3.6	−0.2
21%–30%	3.3	−1.0
11%–20%	2.7	−1.6
Poorest 10%	1.7	−2.1

Note: Change in average additional life expectancy (in years) at age 55 by income between cohorts born in 1920 and 1940.
Sources: Zumbrun (2014).

initiate a local bond market beyond banks), global equity index funds (not to exceed 40% of the asset pool), and the potential for local infrastructure investments (limited to, say, 20% of the asset pool at all times). Although local infrastructure investments would certainly pose conflicts and governance challenges, the long-term investment fit and potential societal productivity gains make them a worthwhile consideration.

#3. Personal Retirement Savings. Personal responsibility is the final "first principle." In Chapter 2, I noted that safety nets require some degree of economic growth and growth requires productivity enhancement. In short, individuals must be encouraged to work and save—to take responsibility. Enter the need for a retirement savings program to preserve, if not grow, our civic capital. The program must be effective and efficient in the way it promotes and allows for savings from all individuals in a society. DC plans both complement DB plans and augment retirement survivability.

Although numerous perspectives are available on what makes the "best" retirement plan structure, too many are normative economic perspectives (i.e., they *should* do so and so) and too few are positive economic perspectives (they actually *would* do so and so). For example, the DB pension is often touted as a far better structure than DC plans. Mathematically (i.e., normatively), pensions are, indeed, the most efficient way to deliver a dollar of lifetime income to retired individuals. Why then have so many private and public pensions failed or come close to failing in recent years? The size and diversity of the participant pools matters. So too does the retiree-to-worker ratio, and this ratio has worsened over time, in part because of the incentive to retire that DB plans provide.

Employers (businesses and government entities) do not last forever, and even if communities do, the community tax base may not. Local economies and tax districts may grow or shrink in terms of employment, income, and tax potential (counting income, property, and sales tax) over time. Moreover, businesses may continue to exist but change locations, causing a group of people to become unemployed and taxes to go uncollected. Yet, the benefit payments have been guaranteed.

Finance professionals have tended to agree that guaranteed benefits in the face of rapidly changing business and tax conditions are inappropriate.[38] In this particular survey, 45% of respondents to a *CFA Institute Financial NewsBrief*

---

[38]*CFA Institute Financial NewsBrief* poll results, answering the question: "What's the primary cause of the underfunded status of US public pension plans?" (13 March 2014): https://blogs.cfainstitute.org/investor/2014/03/13/poll-whats-the-primary-cause-of-the-underfunded-status-of-us-public-pension-plans.

poll think that benefit packages are overly generous. Indeed, the agency conflict associated with politicians who curry favor with workers by promising unaffordable pensions is certainly an important factor. The remaining respondents voted in the following way: weak plan management [using actual poll wording for consistency] (25%), flawed accounting standards (11%), unfavorable demographics (9%), poor capital market returns (5%), and other (5%).

By definition, the "best" structure must be durable and cannot be prone to breakage. Excepting sovereign-scaled plans, the final nails in the DB coffin are:[39]

- Lack of sponsor interest. How many newer companies offer DB pensions? Almost none.

- Portability. How many employees remain with their employer companies beyond 10 years and would be in a position to earn a vested DB pension if one were offered? Almost none. Because DC plans are fully portable, they offer a real advantage to employees.

- "Surplus" risk. The quotation marks indicate that the so-called surplus (assets minus liabilities) is a negative number, a deficit, for most DB plans. Pension liabilities are tantamount to being guaranteed, whereas both asset performance results and plan contributions are anything but guaranteed (contributions are not guaranteed because of contribution "holidays"). In addition, the pensions are even more underfunded in economic reality than they appear on paper according to pension accounting, which understates the liability and exaggerates expected asset returns.

DB pensions may be conceptually best for recipients, but they all too often become risky liabilities for businesses and governments. To the extent that benefit cuts are unavoidable, personal responsibility becomes, unfortunately, very real and necessary.

Personal responsibility simply represents individuals saving; that is what a DC plan is—a savings plan, usually with financial assistance and the supervision of the employer. **Figure 20** provides a set of "second principles" for the range of DC-styled programs to guide us to the best DC structure.

In today's various IRA (individual retirement account) plans, the individual is responsible for opening, contributing to, and managing the account. Although this approach has by far the most flexibility and helps to maintain market integrity through decentralized and (hopefully) independent

---

[39]No final nails for a new plan can be hammered in until plans, beneficiaries, and their constituencies are in agreement on the necessary and permanent changes to be made to "solve" any severe underfunded status. My views are specific (local) to the necessary steps toward sustainability. Although these views do not necessarily fit this "global" book, the views are often requested. My approach is provided in **Appendix 2**.

Figure 20. DC Plan Characteristics

Benefits Illustration	Individual Retirement Savings Account	Employer-Based Retirement System	Societalwide System (e.g., superannuation)
Coverage			→ Most
Ease of Use			→ Easiest
Individual Responsibility	Greatest ←		
Customizable/ Flexible	Most ←		
Pricing Leverage			→ Greatest
Annuity Pricing			→ Lowest
Fiduciary Behavior of Service Providers			→ Greatest
Market(s) Integrity	Greatest ←		

investment, it requires the most preexisting investment knowledge.[40] The individual also has, by definition, the least pricing leverage for products used because of the small account sizes.

The employer-based DC system shown in Figure 20 enables the participant to access professional-quality investment decisions and greater pricing leverage than an IRA (although access to either is not guaranteed). It also demands less of the participant, in terms of preexisting investment knowledge, than individual plans. In addition, the reduction in flexibility in DC plans (when compared with individual investing) is not necessarily, given the lack of investment literacy and research findings that choice can hurt the quality of investment decisions, a bad thing.[41] Employers also often contribute to the individual's account. Employers can also leverage the plan design's structure to promote beneficial behavior through defaults that set up participants to succeed (Falk 2002, Johnson and Goldstein 2003): auto-enrollment, auto-escalating savings rates, and premixed diversified investment funds.

---

[40]Market integrity is critically important, but there are trade-offs. For example, index funds offer investors minimal costs and high levels of diversification, but if too many dollars (threshold unknown) become indexed, markets lose price discovery and capital formation is negatively affected. Based on the public's lack of financial literacy, the ideas proposed in this book favor low cost/high diversification plans. This trade-off may require further exploration than is possible in this book.

[41]For example, see Iyengar and Lepper (2000), Iyengar (2003), and Schwartz (2004).

Arguably, the biggest negative in the employer approach, if defaults are used, is the risk of leakage. Leakage is defined as savings that are spent instead of being rolled over into an IRA or the *next* employer's plan upon separating from an employer. Although leakage could be eliminated through plan designs that do not allow cashing out, such a solution might discourage employees from participating at all, particularly young workers who have few assets but do have job uncertainty and do not want to lock up their savings.

Required contributions into a sovereign-level DC plan (a societalwide system sometimes called a superannuation plan, such as the Australian system) can benefit both employers and individuals, as Figure 20 shows. This system conquers the biggest negative of the employer DC system (leakage) and has greater pricing leverage than any individual or employer plan. Potential drawbacks include (1) the greater government influence over and access to large asset pools and (2) the potential negative impact on market integrity (arguably the most important drawback). To help maintain market integrity and protect individuals from themselves, here are some investment design considerations for a sovereign-level DC plan:

- The plan needs to have a simple structure that can assist all participants regardless of their investment knowledge. The plan should have three tiers: a diversified default in Tier 1; index fund choices in Tier 2; and a brokerage window (perhaps registered funds only) in Tier 3.

- The diversified tier could resemble global balanced funds (Falk 2011a). A better alternative would be a personalized managed account that would be constructed using the individual's age and gender; account balance, contribution, and income levels; and other assets. In other assets would be vested pension projections, including their social security/first pillar assets, with the expected retirement date and other variables taken into account. I designed such an algorithm-based managed account system in collaboration with an actuary in 1999.

Whether to augment either of the previous strategies by investing in strategies other than capitalization-weighted indexes is an important question. Because the number of investable dollars is large, capitalization-weighted indexes minimize costs and maximize diversification. Could companies with actively managed investments validate their abilities and compete for portions of these assets? Possibly, but if this strategy is desired, standards would need to be created and the offerings continually reviewed to ensure that the character of each offering meets the investment goals and is consistent with market integrity.

- Access to the second and third tiers (and a potentially less diversified account) would be limited to individuals who pass a financial literacy test. The rationale for such a "safety first" approach is shown in research, such as Mitchell and Lusardi (2015), who found that financial literacy is sorely lacking among the US populace (see **Figure 21**), and Morningstar, which has conducted its "Mind the Gap" studies annually for years. Comparing the average dollar invested in a fund with the fund's time-weighted returns, Morningstar has found that, across styles (and time), investor buy/sell decisions, on average, detract from performance and tend to do so even more within more volatile categories or cyclical periods. By chasing performance, investors underperform the funds they invest in. Buy-and-hold index funds (and diversified funds, to an even greater extent) help to minimize "bad" behavior.

The second and third tiers would have two restrictions: At least 50% of the account must remain in Tier 2, and the financial literacy test would need to be retaken every three years.

- The ability to allocate among a select group of annuity products (pricing would need to be prenegotiated) could be added to the menu of Tier 2

Figure 21. Financial Literacy Scores by Age Group: Number of Financial Literacy Questions Answered Correctly Out of 10 (2011)

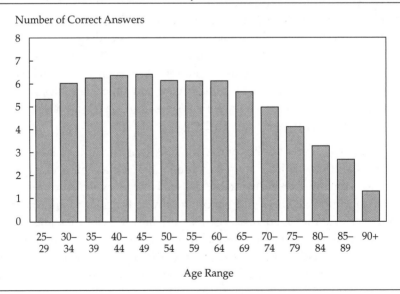

Source: Data are from Texas Tech University and the University of Missouri.

choices. After all, if the goal is to have retirement income, why not offer such solutions that align perfectly with the goal? Keep in mind, however, that for many investors, the sovereign-level DB plan may satisfy the need for a guaranteed lifetime income. Investors wanting even more guaranteed income would have to move beyond the Tier 1 default system. No default approach could properly discern that desire.

Although many sovereign DC plans mandate significant contribution levels by employers and individuals (e.g., 10% each), a strong sovereign DB safety net (e.g., US Social Security or its equivalent) may enable mandated contribution levels to be lower—say, 6% each. Regardless, the plan would require mandatory payroll contributions. The account value will always and without exception be the sole property of the individual (to help protect against government "reach"), and job changes would not require any individual activity.

The most sensible DC design is superannuation, which is a sovereign mandatory savings scheme with personal savings accounts that are invested in markets. It has advantages over strictly individual or employer programs. The investment design protocols could be as easy as the points I have mentioned. Because the accumulated assets include individual contributions, those dollars (*ex* investment gains) could be available for early retirement use by that individual.

With a properly fitted retirement age, a durable safety net, and personal savings, retirement would be enabled for society. However, "enabled" represents only the asset side of the retirement balance sheet; it is really the liability side of the balance sheet that provides a red versus yellow or green light to retire. Specifically, if you have your spending largely under control upon retirement—little to no debt (including mortgage payments) and have largely affordable fixed expenses (as related to your safety-net stipends), such as monthly cable and phone bills—you can think green.

Now that society finds your retirement plan acceptable and you have a green light, is there anything else to worry about? Or is it all now just rainbows and unicorns?

It Is Your Life. Now what? Just because you *can* retire does not mean you *should* retire. Will you be happy? No one can define happiness to everyone's satisfaction, but retirement does not always fit everyone's idea of happiness:

> Flexible work time and retirement options are a potential solution for the challenges of unemployment, aging populations, and unsustainable pension systems around the world. Voluntary part-time workers in Europe and the

US are happier, experience less stress and anger, and are more satisfied with their jobs than other employees. Late-life workers, meanwhile, have higher levels of well-being than retirees. (Graham 2014, p. 1)

Additionally, Robinson (2013) finds:

Research suggests it is those fortunate folks who have little or no excess time, and yet seldom feel rushed, who are happy . . . So, feeling less rushed does not automatically increase happiness . . . Surveys continue to show the least happy group to be those who quite often have excess time. Boredom, it seems, is burdensome . . . high levels of happiness held steady after a long list of demographic factors was taken into account, including marriage, age, education, race and gender. Clearly, there's much to be said for living a productive life at a comfortable pace.

Then again, who said retirement has to be a sedate period or even be devoid of work (part time, of course)? Life expectancy today is such that retirement often has three periods: the go-go start when freedom reigns, the slow-go period when agedness begins to take effect, and the no-go period (hello, couch, hopefully, rather than a hospital bed). In fact, research has indicated a "smile pattern" to the way retirees spend, with higher spending in the go-go period because of travel and other interests, lower spending in the slow-go period, and then higher spending in the no-go period because of health care costs (Blanchett 2013).

Health, unsurprisingly, is a huge factor in older individuals' levels of happiness. As a result, perhaps we need to understand more about how retirement can affect health:

Rates of heart attack and stroke among men and women in the ongoing U.S. Health and Retirement Study [reveal that] those who had retired were 40% more likely to have had a heart attack or stroke than those who were still working. The increase was more pronounced during the first year after retirement, and leveled off after that. (Moon et al. 2012, p. 4)

Now that you may have survived your first year, know that:

Individuals with adequate social relationships have a 50% greater likelihood of survival compared to those with poor or insufficient social relationships. The magnitude of this effect is comparable with quitting smoking and it exceeds many well-known risk factors for mortality (e.g., obesity, physical inactivity). (Smith, Holt-Lunstad, and Layton 2010, p. 14)

And, to reiterate the benefits of relationships:

Loneliness has twice as great an impact on early death as obesity does . . . The effect of loneliness on premature death is nearly as strong as the impact of disadvantaged socioeconomic status, which . . . increases the chances of dying early by 19%. (Cacioppo 2010)

Maybe some continued work is not such a bad idea even if your finances do not require it. Interestingly, many people have already intuited the benefits of continued work and have chosen to delay retirement for reasons beyond additional income (Deevy 2013). The reasons to keep working include, in no specific order: (1) it helps avoid social isolation, (2) it gives meaning to one's life, (3) it allows the use of one's knowledge and experience, (4) it helps maintain one's health, and (5) it is a source of pleasure.

Businesses lose assets (the accumulated knowledge and experience of seasoned employees) when employees retire. By enabling employees to work longer, businesses can reduce this loss and manage better transitions of responsibility and skill to younger workers who will eventually take over from those in gradual or staged retirement. Got succession? Got talent development?

Let's retire the retirement approach of those who came before us. It is time, and we now know better.

Today's Retirement Planning To-Do's (if you must)

This section highlights those things to think about when you are planning retirement today.

#1. Plan Way Ahead. No less than 15–20 years prior to your expected retirement, seek counsel (which could exclude investment advice) from a qualified, fee-only financial planner or adviser.

#2. What Will You Retire to? First and foremost, think about what you will retire to. If you cannot answer this question and will only be retiring *from* something, stop and think about what is next before you begin to plan your retirement.

- Caution—you do not know what you are retiring to until you and your spouse or partner agree. Remember: "I do," for richer or poorer, for better or worse, in sickness and in health . . . but maybe not for lunch. Your new lifestyle could involve being in your spouse's presence 24/7 and include 365 lunches. Can your marriage survive that? Marriage counseling could be among the wisest investments *prior* to your retirement. **Figure 22** shows that divorce in the United States is more than twice as common among those aged 65 and up as it was in 1990. Do not let this drama become a horror show for you. The loss of half of one's savings would make most retirements difficult to finance.

Figure 22. Divorce of Those Aged 50+ on the Rise in the United States

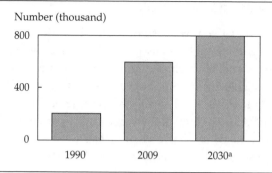

^aProjected.
Source: Brown and Lin (2013).

Caution—retirement can be bad for your health. Do you possess active interests (Boyle et al. 2009), relationships, and a purpose (Yu et al. 2015)? Are you able and prepared to pursue these interests?

- Know that retirement is easier to finance when delayed until your safety net is maximized. Incentives for postponed retirements are sensible.

#3. What Are Your Individual Financial Circumstances? Many rules (and rules of thumb) will tell you how much to save and how to invest it, but be highly skeptical of such rules. Rules of thumb and formulaic approaches do not take into account your personal circumstances. Moreover, using one's individual circumstances in planning is especially important because most savers' situations begin to diverge materially after age 40. Regardless, save (start early), diversify your investments, and see #6 for more.

#4. Recognize the Trade-Offs and Risks. Appreciate that retirement planning is all about trade-offs. If your path toward retirement will not get you all the way there, then you have these four trade-offs to choose from: (1) You can start to save more (live less) today, (2) you can plan to work longer and delay retirement, (3) you can plan to retire on less, or (4) you can take more risk with your investments (and hope for the best) versus saving more. Never forget Robert Burns's advice: "The best laid schemes o' Mice an' Men gang aft agley" (in "To a Mouse"). Please recognize that just because you plan to work longer does not mean that you will be able to, and greater investment risk is not guaranteed to produce greater results. The good news is that the four trade-offs can be combined to really further your path, for example, save a bit more and retire a bit later.

#5. Prepare Your Documents and Your Family/Friends. Execute your "papers" and communicate your wishes with friends and family. At a minimum, provide your attorney's contact information with instructions such as "in case of such-and-such happening to me, contact Mr./ Ms. X." Your papers should include a will, a health care power of attorney, and a power of attorney for property and other financial transactions. Make sure that you discuss with family members (and document the discussion) your desires and expectations for assistance if and when you may need their help. Considering **Table 8** and **Table 9**, draw up specific instructions for dealing with concerns about your cognitive functions

As Tables 8 and 9 show, at the age of 70, a combined 20% of individuals are no longer equipped to make decisions. At age 80, that percentage approaches 50%.

You may even want your documents to include how decision-making assistance would be compensated. The following statistics (Benz 2014) make the point even if the data in Tables 8 and 9 can be challenged:

- Eighty percent of long-term care is provided by unpaid caregivers at home.

- Ten percent of unpaid caregivers go from full-time to part-time work because of their care-giving responsibilities. This issue of compensation

Table 8. Prevalence of Dementia in North America by Age

Age Range	Percentage	Change from Younger Age Range
60–64	0.8%	
65–69	1.7	2.1×
70–74	3.3	1.9
75–79	6.5	2.0
80–84	12.8	2.0
85+	30.1	2.4

Source: Ferri et al. (2005).

Table 9. Cognitive Impairment without Dementia in the United States by Age

Age Range	Percentage
71–79	16.0%
80–89	29.2
90+	38.8

Source: Plassman et al. (2008)

for caregiving can be divisive among siblings who need to care for a parent even when documents exist, let alone when they do not.

#6. What Is Your Spending Plan? Do some math (sorry, but it *is* your retirement). First, your spending plan has two parts: fixed expenses and aspirational spending. Review your current budget and do the following:

- Deduct all expenses that will be gone when you retire. They include retirement plan contributions, related employment taxes, child-related costs (for most people), work-related costs, and your mortgage payment (if your home will not be paid off, strongly consider a move into a home that can be paid for in full or do not retire yet).

- Add in an estimate for out-of-pocket health care costs (copayments, deductibles, etc.) and count them as a fixed expense, even though the expense will be variable. Costs will vary significantly from country to country and often do not include estimates for long-term care (LTC).

Does your country have "filial piety" laws—under which children must provide some parental care or face penalties? Or will your children simply accept a role to provide assistance as related to #5?

Recent research in the United States may moderate some of the fears of high LTC costs.[42] The likelihood of need remains high, but the costs may be manageable by using (instead of costly and risky LTC insurance) savings, home equity, or even a life insurance policy with an LTC rider: The average stay in a care facility for a man is under a year (44% likelihood of need after age 65); the average stay for a woman in a facility is 17 months (58% likelihood of need after age 65). Moreover, 45% of patients stay fewer than three months. The probability of a stay of five years or longer is not, however, insignificant—7% for women and 2% for men. Thus, the distribution of LTC costs is very "right tailed," with few people paying significantly above-average costs. Based on this observation, one LTC policy *hope* for today is that policies will offer longer waiting periods (i.e., one year or even longer) to cover the tail risk and lower the costs.

If you want to make a bequest and it is not solely "whatever is left," then you may want to pursue a life insurance policy and add in the life insurance costs to the fixed costs. Life insurance may be a cheaper and more guaranteed bequest tool.

---

[42]Friedberg et al. (2014). Note that these results are very different from prior industry reports because of the ability to see monthly versus annual data.

- Split the remaining expenditure estimates into fixed and aspirational columns. Note that certain expenses, such as food, can be both fixed and aspirational and should be split. For example, steak might be aspirational whereas hamburger is fixed. Always and everywhere, the smaller your fixed expenses, the easier it will be for you to retire.

Next, "immunize before you (try to) optimize."[43] *Immunized* simply means having your fixed expenses covered by guaranteed payments, such as your safety net, or pension stipends. Immunizing your fixed expenses also means that nonsafety-net, residual savings can be theoretically invested in any way desired, regardless of volatility. With immunization, your retirement is safe for as long as you live and mostly independent—other than health care shocks—from whatever happens in the markets.

If your fixed expenses are more than your (expected) safety net or pension stipends, then you could purchase an annuity[44] or laddered bond portfolio with your savings to shore up the gap. You may also want to consider how you might monetize a large asset that many possess: a home. Techniques to tap home equity, such as additional guaranteed payments, can help ease the financing of retirement without having to purchase an annuity. Moreover, immunized fixed expenses reduce sequence risk (the need to sell investments during a bad market cycle), which improves the longevity of the invested residual savings because they can be invested for longer. Let the investment results from your invested residual savings feed your aspirational (discretionary) expenditures. In strongly positive investment years, you will eat even better. In less positive years or down-market years, your expenditures should be on a diet (Waring and Siegel 2015). An unfortunate reality is that too many people have fixed expenses that are too large a percentage (e.g., >50%) of their total expenditures and have yielded control of their lifestyle to the vagaries of investments.

#7. Consider Part-Time Work. Consider part-time work if your savings and desired lifestyle numbers do not balance particularly well (or if you simply want some of the pleasures of work and its social aspects).

---

[43]This phrase was coined in 2009 by the author and used in many speeches and interviews—for example, see www.morningstar.com/cover/videocenter.aspx?id=651935.

[44]Annuities come in many shapes and sizes. This reference highlights the ability to purchase monthly lifetime income. The income can begin immediately or be deferred to begin later. Deferred annuities—such as those that begin payments at expected mortality (e.g., longevity insurance)—can be valuable planning tools because they cost much less (e.g., 15% of an immediate annuity's cost) and still insure that longevity. And although annuity contracts guarantee lifelong monthly income, the guarantee is only as good as the guarantor, or the insurance, backing them. Default risk, albeit small, always exists.

- Work where you spend money. The discount can only help. It is even better if the work connects with a hobby or interest. For example, golf course employment could allow for free rounds.

- Income from this work could delay all needs to purchase any immunization products, and you may want to save such purchases for when there is a full retirement.

Although there are many sophisticated ways in which to do this type of planning, the framework presented here is foundational. Keep in mind that simple is less fragile than complex. Be wary of overly sophisticated plans and their many assumptions.

4. A Cure for Health Care

The only way to keep your health is to eat what you don't want, drink what you don't like, and do what you'd rather not.

—Mark Twain, Following the Equator, *1897*

What a way to begin a chapter with the words "health care" in the title! We eat what we want, drink what we like, and generally fall short on those things we should do, such as regularly exercising. Insurance and social policies exist to treat illness and injury, not generally for *health* care. Would they not be more appropriately labeled *sick* or *injured* care policies?

We do not always keep ourselves healthy. As a result, the sick care industry is quite healthy and growing. Unfortunately, the pace of its growth crowds out other social expenditures. That growth can also seriously damage worker participation and deplete individual retirement plans. The sick care industry's growth trajectory might just make you ill (unless you are part of the industry).

Developed economies have their demographic and longevity challenges, whereas developing economies struggle with the availability of care, poor sanitation, diseases, poor air quality, and global environmental change. The costs of health care, as delivered today, are too high if our goal is sustainable growth. Consider, for example, the alleged "simple" solution—for people to work longer. This solution works only to the extent people are physically able (and jobs are also available). Improved longevity means a longer life, but it does not necessarily mean an increased health span; morbidity (lack of wellness) is also on the rise.

Until and unless we shift to health care policies with the actual goal of increasing health spans, we will all have to deal with society's higher health care costs as well as our own health costs because of ever greater demand and, in many parts of the world, limited supply. True "health care" needs to include incentives that bias people toward earlier detection of illness, healthier behavior, and improved access to care. If we want to realign the economics to be sustainable, personal responsibility must be a part of any policy. According to the Chopra Foundation,

> In the last decade or so mounting research has shown how lifestyle changes, including exercise, stress management, and diet can prevent almost ninety percent (90%) of chronic illnesses in our society. It is now known that only five percent (5%) of disease-related gene mutations are fully penetrant. In other words, the gene expression of these mutations cannot be stopped unless a future drug or technology is developed to stop that expression. In most of

the other gene-related mutations related to chronic disease, lifestyle can affect gene expression. We now know that Type 2 diabetes, cardiovascular illness in general, and many types of cancer are preventable. In addition almost every chronic disease is related to inflammation in the body and can be ameliorated through modified gene expression. ("State of Health" 2014)

Current approaches create high-cost sick care systems because they do not deal with life styles. This statement is true for both single-payer systems and multipayer systems. Multipayer systems add additional cost problems because of fragmented responsibilities. Neither of these systems can walk away from the economic risks that are here today, let alone the greater risks we face tomorrow, unless a change occurs. Let's learn how to improve our own health—and the health of our economies. We only get one body; maybe we should learn how to best care for it.

First Principles for Health Care Policy

Any framework for sustainable health care policies begins with a robust, core structure (such as DNA[45]). The material that follows in this chapter includes additional perspectives and research details about 10 components (pieces) needed to help complete/solve the health care puzzle.

1. Insurance coverage makes sense for *insurable risks* (principally, risks with a low probability of occurring but a high cost if they occur).[46] Health maintenance and acute needs are best covered differently. Coverage that differentiates between maintenance and acute needs would be more affordable and allow for sustainable support of what many consider an inalienable right.

2. To properly link the user and payer of services, all policy or uninsured costs would need to be the *responsibility of the individual* or the person's guardian. Services could be broadly defined to include the use of physician or facility time, facility tools, and equipment or medication.

3. All coverages would be *individually owned*; coverage could never be lost.

4. Coverage(s) would include *minimum use requirements* to promote health maintenance and promote health.

---

[45]DNA contains the instructions used in the development and functioning of all known living organisms.

[46]In the theory of insurance, an insurable risk is one for which an insurance pool can be constructed so that those who do not suffer a loss help to pay the losses of those who do. Most, but not all, insurable risks involve a low probability of occurrence and a high amount of loss conditional on the loss occurring.

5. *Supplemental coverage(s)* could be made available to allow individuals to customize their own coverage to accommodate their individual behavior, needs, and concerns.

6. To the extent feasible, services provided would be priced *in consideration of outcomes*, not solely based on fee-for-service pricing. Although outcome-based pricing would be the goal, the effect of such a system on the supply of doctors and other medical providers would need to be considered, perhaps making it necessary to accept some fee-for-service pricing.

7. Costs of all services, devices, and patient experiences would be *fully transparent*.

8. *Intelligent access* to assistance would be available with any medical professional anywhere and anytime there is need, and coordinated care would become the norm. Preferred or required networks for care would no longer exist.

9. *Technology, records, and information* would become the "central medical nervous system" for the entire medical system and be leveraged to act as the facilitator of information and timely feedback to caregivers and patients.

10. The internet could be used to leverage specific *charitable pools and tools* to fund, for example, "orphan drug" programs or to enhance the affordability of coverage via donations to specialty clinics.[47] Such donations might qualify for an estate tax exemption, as described in Appendix 1.

Key to the success of these principles is the interaction of the incentives and personal responsibility.

- *Incentives* would be offers that could improve health, such as inoculations, checkups, prescriptions (in hand) after hospital stays, or perhaps even gym memberships (when used). Such incentives need to become typical and free of additional charges. **Figure 23** shows that, globally, the adoption of health care products drops precipitously in response to very small fees. According to the Abdul Latif Jameel Poverty Action Lab (2011),

> Policies often set the prices of preventive health care products low to promote access while also providing a revenue stream to providers. But if access is important, it makes sense to bring the price all the way down to zero. A series of evaluations finds that even small price increases above zero lead to large drops in the number of people who choose to buy health products. (Figure 8.2)

---

[47]An orphan drug is one that has been developed specifically to treat a rare ("orphan") medical condition.

69

Figure 23. Adoption of Health Care Products

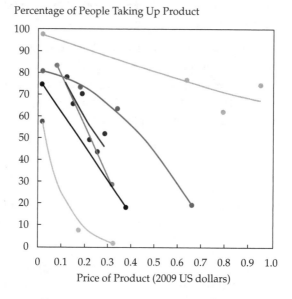

Percentage of People Taking Up Product

Price of Product (2009 US dollars)

- Deworming Kenya
- Bed nets in clinics, Kenya
- Bed net vouchers, Kenya
- Water disinfectant, Zambia
- Water disinfectant, Kenya
- Soap, India

Source: Abdul Latif Jameel Poverty Action Lab (2011): Figure 8.2.

The best goal for any and all incentives is for them to passively nudge us toward our own wellness, but sometimes the nudge needs to be a shove. You would think we had enough incentive within ourselves, if only as a result of having only one body and knowing how health affects our happiness. But we clearly do not. Let's finally drive a stake into the heart of *Homo economicus*, for those who still believe.

Surcharges should be used for unwanted behavior, such as smoking.

- *Personal responsibility*: Increased wellness can help manage costs, but wellness is also good for the individual. If we can create an incentive for wellness, a win-win-win outcome is possible because individuals who take responsibility will be healthier, work attendance and quality will increase, and the health care system will become stronger (i.e., through a network effect).[48] As

---

[48]The classic example of a network effect is the telephone. The more people who own telephones, the more valuable the telephone is to each owner. This effect creates a positive externality because a user may purchase a telephone without intending to create value for other users but does so in any case.

a result, our economies will become more robust and, dare we claim, more sustainable. In addition, fewer people will be disabled, so there will be more workers and fewer dependents. Individuals would need to agree to specific responsibilities, however, such as regular checkups with medical professionals and pay additional fees for behavior detrimental to wellness. The individual would need to be the center of all policy initiatives (per the third principle concerning *individually owned policies*).

#1. Insurable Risks/Affordability. If you drive, you probably have a car insurance policy in case of an accident. Such a policy makes good sense if the annual cost of the insurance is a low percentage of your income, but it makes less sense if the cost is more than 10% of your income. Why would a policy ever be so expensive? Horrible driver records aside, policies would be much more costly if the insurance company needed to cover vehicle maintenance (oil changes, brake pad replacements, new tires, etc.) because of the checks they would be guaranteed to have to write. Because maintenance is not included in car insurance policies, the cost of these policies makes sense. Interestingly, vehicle *manufacturers* have begun to include (some) maintenance in their "deals" when an individual purchases or leases a vehicle. Why? It helps to sell the car, but more importantly, it helps to ensure that the vehicles will operate better for longer—which helps to maintain higher used-vehicle prices and benefits dealers.[49] Hmm . . . better for longer?

So, with our "one body for life," why does the goal to make health insurance affordable not make better sense? To enable greater affordability and pursue "better for longer" for ourselves, we need to become responsible for our maintenance costs plus our costs of use up to a somewhat uncomfortable threshold (i.e., an annual deductible—for example, 5% of the median income per year[50]). All risks and needs—medical, dental, and mental—greater than the annual deductible would be the responsibility of an insurer in this example. And costs pertaining to an ongoing ailment (year over year) would not require any further deductible payments. As it pertains to the older age cohorts, LTC coverage premiums could even be priced into the deductible but only when the need carries beyond five years. Just as car dealers benefit by including some maintenance in the purchase price, health insurers would benefit if maintenance were included at little to no cost to the consumer as a

---

[49]A question remains as to whether dealers will be able to benefit enough. Apart from how "better for longer" vehicles also could decrease future demand, we may want to consider today's oversupply in light of an ever-increasing supply of driver services and the forthcoming robo-cars. How many hours per day do you drive your car on average? As on-demand transportation becomes ever more available, personal ownership could become less desirable.
[50]In the United States, this is roughly $2,500, or 5% of roughly $50,000.

way to mitigate the insurers' longer-term, more costly exposure(s). Such high deductibles should be set to help promote affordability and to correspond with specific age cohorts because of the varied needs we all have at different points in our lives. Following is an illustration of how deductibles and coverage might vary by age cohort:

- The age cohort of *birth to age five* typically has specific and limited health needs, such as checkups and vaccinations. This period of care has a profound impact, however, on the child's long-term growth and cognition. Proper health care during this period is a primary factor that drives equality of opportunity in life; creates a long-term, positive healthy life style; and boosts productivity. Recognizing, additionally, that the child has no resources of his own and that his parents are typically starting out in their careers, ideal coverage would be the lowest premium cost and lowest deductible.

- The age cohort of *age 6 to age 20-something* has needs primarily related to illness or injury, with few serious health incidences. Ideal coverage for this group would be the lowest premium and midlevel deductible.

- An age cohort of *20-something to 40-something* has needs largely related to wellness maintenance and some early detection. If we regard this age cohort as being the most likely to have young children and to include new mothers, then note that prenatal and postnatal health is another primary factor in opportunity equality. Ideal coverage for this group would be midlevel premium costs and the midlevel deductible.

- The age cohort of *late 40s until retirement* has needs that are becoming more expansive; early detection is becoming relevant, and costs are beginning to rise. Note that this age cohort coincides (roughly) with one's peak earning years. Ideal coverage would be the highest premium cost and highest deductible.

- Upon *retirement*, the deductible matters less to insurers than their maximum exposure. This point will be covered in more detail in #2 (Individual Responsibility). Ideal coverage would be the highest premium cost and midlevel deductibles.

As noted, deductibles could rise and fall over time on the basis of the age cohort, as would the costs of coverage. Regardless, the use of any age cohort to help support another, other than dependent children, should be avoided and might even be prohibited. To make health care policy sustainable, each cohort must be primarily responsible for itself. (Note that this stricture also applies to some countries' pharmaceutical costs being subsidized by others.)

With the use of high-deductible coverage, individuals should have the ability to open and maintain their own dedicated-use HSAs. These accounts should be encouraged via tax-favored contributions, growth, and tax-free expenditures when used for health care or coverage-related expenses, including prescriptions. This consumer-driven form of coverage has been shown to decrease claims and costs (when prices matter, overuse decreases) while maintaining quality.[51]

The HSA could even be a home for a new type of government bond dedicated to HSA use, which could be inflation-linked to the health care industry's inflation rate or could include a dedicated investment pool for health care technology and research as well as other, more typical investments. Might such HSA bonds engender more government oversight of the health care industry because of the potential for inflated costs? And might they negate some of the industry's "capture" of the regulatory system through extensive lobbying efforts (at least in the United States)?[52] Because HSAs offer a tax benefit, they should have an annual contribution limit relative to the deductible in any given year—say, a contribution to the HSA no larger than three times the deductible—and the HSA should also have a maximum account limit (e.g., 20 times the annual deductible) beyond which contributions would no longer be permitted.

For individuals who are unable to afford their coverage or deductible in any given year, the HSA could be a conduit for governmental assistance. HSAs would be "fundable" through any combination of employer contributions, a relative's help, or government assistance as an annual backstop in the event that an HSA falls short of funds. Separately, an employer could offer additional benefits to help individuals manage their costs with the offer of wellness classes or gym access. In addition, employers could offer lower negotiated rates for access to nutritionists, trainers, and other health practitioners. The government could even provide an annual HSA contribution to individuals below certain income thresholds. Remember that, without chronic illness or disability, an HSA should grow over time, which would lessen the need for government assistance. When you consider that the HSA of a child, with typically low health needs, would benefit from the magic of compound interest for a long time, accumulated HSA balances could be a lot of help. Governments could even offer "birthday contributions" to the HSA accounts of young children. Might fertility rates get a nudge?

#2. Individual Responsibility. Why make the individual responsible? Consider the aforementioned car insurance; the driver's prior experience

---

[51]Gusland, Harshey, Schram, and Swim (2010).
[52]"Capture" is defined as influence that is inappropriate in light of the public interest.

affects the cost of insurance. If individuals are allowed to eat and drink as much as they want, not exercise, smoke, and participate in dangerous activities (such as skydiving or motorcycle racing) yet have the same costs as their healthy contemporaries, then why not just enjoy ourselves? Such a free-rider scenario increases the costs for everyone but less so for the individual free rider. Individuals should be responsible for the following:

- To cover (or arrange for) payment of any coverage and deductible costs when needed or make good on any costs incurred—if payments are missed—over time.

- To accept potential age-cohort cost variations born from good and bad behavior. Cost increases or decreases from the cohort average (based on measures or tests) would be restricted to a range of ±50%.

- To satisfy any mandated use, election, or information sharing requirements in the policy

- To be involved with their own care (E-Patients.net 2011)

- To accept full financial responsibility for elective health care procedures, such as plastic surgery. The HSA could be used, but the election would not entail any insurer responsibility.

- To provide, as a part of an "in-force" policy, a revocable election as to whether life-saving medical treatment(s) should be provided or withheld at the time of a need.[53] Based on US surveys (Bellucksept 2014), more than 70% of individuals would prefer to die at home. To the extent that people in other countries have similar preferences, health care systems might be able to save significant costs (based on the end-of-life cost estimates coming from medical facilities) by using in-home care.[54]

In a similar vein, various studies have shown how a small percentage (i.e., 5%) of health care users can generate more than half the total costs within a system (Breslow 2012). These users are typically made up of both very young, chronically ill patients and older individuals who are near the end of their lives.

---

[53]In 1991, La Crosse, Wisconsin, medical leaders began a systemic campaign to push medical people and patients to discuss end-of-life (EOL) desires. It then became routine for all patients admitted to a hospital to answer four crucial questions. Each question began with: At this moment in your life . . .? Their answers could change with each admittance. By 1996, 85% of La Crosse residents who died had a written advance directive and EOL costs were half of the national average (Hammes 2012).

[54]I respect that these costs vary survey by survey and are wholly dependent on a given health care system. These estimates, although consistently material, range widely enough to make any specific citation inappropriate.

What follows on this point may unintentionally offend some readers, but the goal is simply to illuminate a most serious and difficult issue. How can an economic system with limited resources justify a large investment in a sick child or a retired, elderly individual? Probably, and sadly, it cannot if the system is to be sustainable. Furthermore, blame for the failure to face this responsibility is shared with the medical community. Consider this quotation by the surgeon and professor Atul Gawande (2014): " . . . our decision making in medicine has failed so spectacularly that we have reached the point of actively inflicting harm on patients rather than confronting the subject of mortality" (p. 178).

This money versus medical (treatment) conundrum could be addressed, in part, by engaging charity to bear the costs and by the dying to refuse life-saving treatment.[55] But what about those who accept treatment and do not receive charitable help? Although denial of treatment does not seem to fit in a society in pursuit of greatness, the issue is a free-rider problem. A suggested fix would be to install a lifetime cap on eligible, insured health care expenditures for those who are either diagnosed with a terminal illness or, for example, those beyond his or her society's life-expectancy age from birth, or some other age criterion.[56]

Of course, individuals and their families would always be allowed to personally finance costs beyond the cap. Such a cap could also include a feature that allowed for up to half of any unused cap amount to be HSA "inheritable" by relatives (up to their own individual limits) or by a charitable pool exclusively used for HSA support of those in need.

Finally, such a policy could boost medical tourism—to make those cap dollars go farther (with the assumption that travel is medically possible). This travel should be fully acceptable by insurers, especially in light of the

---

[55]Maybe it is not such a conundrum. Research (Spettel et al. 2009; Temel et al. 2010) indicates that greater hospice and palliative care may be better choices, with less suffering, fewer costs, and more days with loved ones.

[56]This cap should be decided by a group using data on expenditure exposure and life expectancy; the group should be composed of doctors, nurses, insurers, religious leaders, lawyers, and experts on aging. The best cap might represent a median-like number and could be higher for the young than for the old because of the greater potential for productive capacity among the young with improved health. Perhaps more importantly, we should heed the following from the physician B.J. Miller (2015): "Health care was designed with diseases, not people, at its center. Which is to say, of course, it was badly designed. And nowhere are the effects of bad design more heartbreaking or the opportunity for good design more compelling than at the end of life, where things are so distilled and concentrated. There are no do-overs . . . For most people, the scariest thing about death isn't being dead, it's dying, suffering. It's a key distinction. To get underneath this, it can be very helpful to tease out suffering which is necessary as it is, from suffering we can change."

increase in information flow that would result from greater medical tourism. The quality of care in some lower-cost parts of the world can be excellent. Furthermore, the increased overseas competition for "big-ticket" operations would encourage changes in local markets beneficial to local constituents. Hello, competition!

#3. Individual Ownership. When your coverage begins at birth, by definition, preexisting conditions are minimized and the risks for any insurer are randomized across a society or any large subgroup of it. "Randomized" is a bit overstated, however, because parent histories and prenatal screens could reduce some percentage of risky pregnancies or births. However, it is up to individuals—in the absence of laws[57]—to decide whether, and how, to use such information or take any action.

"Individually owned" simply means that you will always possess the same coverage regardless of whether you are employed. Minors would have their own policies, but one or more guardians (such as parents) would be listed and be responsible for all related costs. Of course, upon the minor's age of majority, the responsibility would become hers or his.

The only possible limitation could be a policy's functionality outside of your country's borders. Your HSA debit account, however, could be used to pay for services anywhere. Those services should also be creditable against your annual deductible regardless of the place of use. Of course, travel insurance could always be used for large risks, and extended stays might simply "connect" to the local health care policies.

#4. Minimum Use Requirements. So, you have but one body. What is the warranty? The warranty would be one of those "to get the best use, do such and such" types of warranties. The challenge is that, even if you follow the instructions (e.g., proper diet, exercise, and brain stimulation), wear and tear happens, as do accidents and illnesses. And some people are born with special needs or with unusual susceptibility to one disease or another. If the system needs to avoid free riders and early detection of health risks helps the system's sustainability, then individuals should be encouraged to tend to their health.

Apart from any future potential technology requirements (see #10 to follow) a no-cost warranty would be included with your coverage. The warranty would both require and include regular physician checkups and physicals at a frequency that is appropriate to your age cohort. If a treatment for a condition is recommended, then it would be required as part of

---

[57]Local laws or regulations may interfere with choice; I strongly recommend that individuals make their own decisions if they are able.

the warranty.[58] Warranty compliance would allow for much greater insight into an individual's health and increase the potential for early detection, be likely to improve health over time, and build population-wide data to facilitate research that could benefit everyone.

Noncompliance, including policy nonpayment, would be costly for the system. As a result, a strong deterrent, such as an increase in deductible liability from $X to $4X, should be applied to years when coverage either does not exist or is out of warranty. Compliance with your physician's suggestions would be between the two of you unless specific treatment is recommended and documented with all the relevant details; if your unhealthy behavior leads to worsened health indicators (e.g., increased blood pressure), however, then the cost of your coverage could go up. Only responsible, not free, riders are welcome.

#5. Supplemental Coverages. The word "supplemental" should not suggest that the primary coverage would be partial. Primary coverage would be all inclusive except for elective surgeries (e.g., cosmetic surgery in the absence of an accident or deformity) and have no lifetime maximum until and unless an insurance cap is triggered. The primary coverage would be paid by all and have no limitations of coverage or restrictions based on religious grounds that exceed the laws of a country. HSAs could be used for any medical-related services or goods, even if elective, and as a result, supplemental coverage would be needed for only large potential liabilities, such as the following:

- A specific policy for individuals to extend their coverage (remove the age cap) or limit their deductible because of a serious concern, such as a worrisome family history of a degenerative disease, could be considered. Concerns about treatment costs, which could continue for years, might spark interest in such a policy. Supplemental coverage might be used to pay out-of-pocket costs for a certain period (e.g., $30,000 plus the coverage costs for 10 years) upon a confirmed diagnosis.

- Third-party coverage might be provided to extend an insurance cap if and when it is reached.

#6. Consideration of Outcomes. If the goal is health, then why are costs tied to anything other than a patient's health outcome? Perhaps we should shine a bit of light on this question before fully exploring this sixth principle. Costs cannot be exclusively linked to outcomes because of the following:

---

[58]If costs are somewhat linked to outcomes and are transparent (see #6 and #7 to follow), then we can hope that recommendations will be made with the only the best intentions.

- Much remains unknown about the human body. Remember that medicine is a "practice," and outcomes cannot be guaranteed.

- The existence of (too?) many tort laws and the reality of human fallibility can make for a type of perverse "lottery" for patients via medical lawsuits. Honest mistakes should not cost doctors and their insurers great sums of money and thereby increase everyone else's costs. These lotteries occur and do so without the advent of outcome-based charges. Without appropriate legal protections, outcome-based charges are a nonstarter. Regardless, the lotteries need to end.

- Medical professionals' time is valuable, and their overhead costs are real but not necessarily linked to outcomes. If you pay your plumber hourly, then what is a clogged artery worth? Do you think that your plumber's tools, truck, and insurance coverage(s) are free? Although overhead costs will never be uniform globally, they would be more similar locally. Professionals could itemize their own "regularly used" list of services and items and publish their "per hour" charge for each.

- A way of fully linking costs to outcomes might seem salutary, but such a complete shift might not be either practical or desirable. Serious diseases with a low but positive probability of a cure (say, leukemia) might go untreated because the chance of getting paid would be low. At the same time, conditions with a high probability of being cured but worthy of only a low price, such as ear infections, could not generate enough outcome-based fees to allow the system to exist or be on call.

To align interests and sustain the industry, we need a blend of "time and materials" and outcome prices. Once transparency (#7) increases, such a blended fee system could become more prominent.[59] Indeed, new models of payment systems are already being tried. **Figure 24** shows, based on an annual survey of 24,000 doctors in 25 specialties, the percentage of physicians participating in nontraditional payment models.

#7. Full Transparency. In the sixth principle, the phrase "time and materials" was borrowed from the construction industry. Odd as it might seem, the cost of time and materials should be the transparency goal for the health care industry. Until we achieve that level of clarity, the economic costs (and prices) of the health care industry will likely continue to cause pain and suffering.

Although some health care providers, such as large hospital complexes (Reinhardt 2013), do not seem to be fully supportive of transparency, the push

---

[59]Could we (should we) hope for the same for actively managed investments—a small flat fee and an incentive fee linked to alpha production or achievement of the desired outcome?

Figure 24. New Models

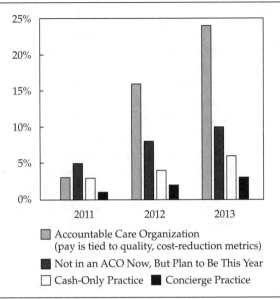

Accountable Care Organization
(pay is tied to quality, cost-reduction metrics)

■ Not in an ACO Now, But Plan to Be This Year
□ Cash-Only Practice ■ Concierge Practice

Note: The percentage of physicians participating in nontraditional payment models, based on an annual survey of 24,000 doctors in 25 specialties.
Source: Medscape Physician Compensation Report (2014).

is spot on. The asymmetry of information in health care—profitable for providers, costly for consumers and taxpayers—may contribute to some of the dislike of price transparency, but the topic is much more complicated than it may seem. Prices are often unclear. For example, a hospital's general overhead could be allocated per room or per patient. So, what's the real marginal cost?[60] The

---

[60]This question often connects, wrongly, with an anti-immigrant and/or anti-uninsured-patient position. The economist Yves Smith (2014) wrote, "I hate to point out something no one likes thinking about: the price of hospital services, which is what critics usually harangue about when talking about the mythical immigrant who shows up with a heart attack, has nothing to do with the marginal cost of providing those services. The only marginal cost to the hospital is the extent to which the person who shows up in the emergency room uses disposables (as in drugs, disinfectants, food, disposables used to process tests, like syringes and lab supplies) and/or takes up a bed when the hospital is at capacity and displaces a presumed paying customer. That is one of the maddening things about the price of hospital services generally, that it is designed to recover large overheads and is even more arbitrary by virtue of insurers having negotiated steep discounts, leaving those unlucky enough not to be consuming discounted services being hit with unjustifiably high prices. Only if there are enough undocumented immigrants who show up at hospitals for the hospital to be forced to add to capacity to deal with them, as in add to their medical staff or increase hospital beds, are these workers affecting the hospital's economics in any meaningful way."

proper price for the "material" use of an MRI (magnetic resonance imaging) machine would seem to be appropriately based on how many scans the machine makes in its life, which is unknown. The challenge of unknown prices can be addressed, up to a point, by a tiered approach to how and where people receive care for their health needs (see #8 to follow).

Another complication arises with achieving transparency. Unless both parties have similar levels of knowledge, which is almost impossible to imagine, full transparency cannot be achieved. But transparency can be improved, starting with genuine competition among the industry players, which would contribute to price discovery. Such competition could be enabled by changes in the influence of the health care industry—in particular, the pharmaceutical companies. But the pharma companies cannot stifle competition by themselves; regulator (referee) capture is a contributor. Here are a few simple, perhaps shameful examples:

- Although the United States funds research on behalf of pharma through the National Institutes of Health, it does not negotiate prices—for Medicare, for example. The norm in some other countries is to negotiate prices and restrict access to pricier drugs unless a clear benefit can be shown. In Australia, the Therapeutic Goods Administration researches drugs, picks one or two in each category deemed the most effective (often not the newest), and concentrates its purchases to secure better prices.

- What have we been paying for? In 2003, Allen Roses, a senior executive for GlaxoSmithKline, announced that the vast majority of drugs, more than 90%, work in only 30%–50% of people (Connor 2003). We could and should, however, expect this to improve with more personalized medicines based on individual genomes.

- Drug companies spend more on advertising and marketing than they do on research (Stiglitz and Greenwald 2014). Huh?!

- And what about the right to choose medicine, Mr. or Ms. Regulator? Let's broaden an individual's right in certain dire medical situations to choose.

With more transparency and less regulatory capture, prices would begin to incorporate a reasonable profit rather than the monopoly-style profits that are sometimes earned in pharma presently. One worthwhile outcome would be a published price list. Before anyone scoffs at the possibility of such an outcome, it is widely seen in the dentistry industry in the United States because most people have little or no dental insurance.

The most typical criticism of consumer-style prices is the inability to "shop" when, for example, someone is en route to an emergency room for treatment. That is a perfectly fair criticism, but most (70% or more) drugs are prescribed for chronic conditions, not emergencies.

#8. Intelligent Access. Whenever you are sick or injured, a care facility should be nearby, available, and accept your insurance. Universal access may be hard to achieve, but that does not mean it is not the right goal. We would benefit from a shift to universal access. The build-out of facilities and tiers to make this possible is as follows:

- A large number of *small, local walk-in clinics*, such as those that currently exist in pharmacies, service minor health needs and questions and are staffed by nurse practitioners. The walk-in system would expand access at a low price and with easily visible costs. Interestingly, this system is already poised to expand and could even also offer tele-doctor access. **Figure 25** shows what a medical kiosk with tele-doctor availability might look like.

- *Numerous small emergency centers* (with limited overnight rooms) for convenient ambulatory access could function as triage facilities for treatment and release or (at worst) stabilization prior to relocation to a hospital.

Figure 25.   Medical Kiosk with Tele-Doctor

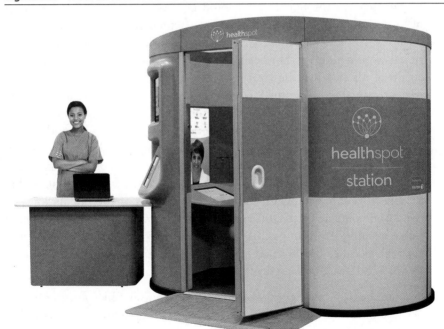

Source: HealthSpot.net.

- *Single-purpose specialty clinics* could leverage their specific skills to take volume away from hospital complexes. Costs become more transparent and lower, and these clinics would also offer greater efficiency and skill (because of higher volumes and specialization) for procedures. A trend in this direction has already started with knee surgeries, rehabilitation clinics, and CT (computerized tomography) and MRI scans (Wu, Sylwestrzak, Shah, and DeVries 2014).

- *Hospitals* would continue to play an important role, but they should become smaller and more focused to increase their ability to understand and control their own costs. Their focus should be on high-risk patients in need of extended stays, who would be patients because of planned surgery or relocation from a local emergency center. Hospitals should distance themselves from one another by at least 80 kilometers (roughly 50 miles), except for those within high-density areas.

If real estate is about location, location, location, then health care should adopt a mantra of access, access, access. Access is more than simply location because it can also denote the type of care and the range of professionals needed.

- Expanded care through teams should become the norm. An advantage of insurance being accepted everywhere (remember that this new system does not include a "preferred" medical network) is that medical professionals would all be part of one system—a team assigned to a patient with access to all records. The ability to leverage cooperation would increase; patient care should improve, if only as a result of fewer communication errors.[61] Furthermore, many clinical problems could be solved by partnering with "upstream groups" (Manchanda 2014), those who understand and address a patient's social and environmental conditions. Housing, the neighborhood, or living and working conditions could be the cause of the patient's symptoms. These teams could also include activities that are likely to enhance health for specific segments of the population . . . (which) lie outside the traditional health care system . . . such as prenatal care, teaching parenting skills, and supporting families during the first years of a child's life—which represent long-term economic investments (Sayer and Lee 2014).

- The numbers and types of professionals needed would likely begin to shift because of this new system or shifts in local demographics. For example:

---

[61]Dishman (2013) noted that 80% of errors with health care professionals and workers occur via communication/organization problems.

- Careers could open up for health care counselors and consultants to help guide the use of HSAs and cost or price research on services. Certified financial planners are available to help people with their finances; let's promote *certified health planners* for people's health to play a role with the upstream professionals. The work could be done on an hourly or on a retainer basis—both HSA eligible.

- More nurse practitioners and physician's assistants, who are already in short supply, would be needed for the walk-in clinics.

- More primary care physicians would be needed to satisfy all of those maintenance warranties. These physicians are the front line of defense, the early detectors, and they serve as the greatest defense against the system's costs.

- More gerontologists, who are also already needed, would be necessary because of aging populations.

The need for specialists—the most expensive cog in the health care machine—could decline as a result of these access changes, the preferred and expanded use of primary care physicians, and the much-needed increased use of gerontologists. Such a change would help manage costs.[62] Would specialists pivot toward the other more "generic" physician roles (which compensate less)? And how might we create incentives to direct future health care workers into the nonspecialist roles? Pay off their student loans? Perhaps educational scholarships could be used to help encourage these positions and fill any gaps.

#9. Leveraging Technology, Records, and Information. Are we near the tipping point, or have we already reached a tipping point in which the technology of real-time information, low-cost memory, and big data are available to leverage wellness? I think yes. As we reach a critical mass of patient information—not only on a given patient, but also on the population of patients with similar attributes—the medical field will be able to use artificial intelligence and large datasets to identify potential medical problems in the future and vastly improve the practice of preventive medicine. This change could have a large impact on changing patients' life styles.

The question is whether improving the practice of preventive medicine will lower health care costs. If DNA analysis is included in that dataset, I believe this change will significantly bend the health care industry's cost

---

[62]In a study by Boult et al. (2001), those who saw the geriatrics team were 25% less likely to become disabled, 50% less likely to become depressed, and 40% less likely to require home health services.

curve. Although this kind of cost relief is debatable, consider the benefits of data collection with real-time health tools, such as a bands and watches, clothing, skin patches, eye contacts, and real-time alerts for strokes, heart attacks, and other major events. If these tools were made part of an insurance policy's warranty, how many long and expensive treatments could be avoided? **Figure 26** shows how text message reminders improved adherence to antiretroviral therapy in a study of HIV-positive and AIDS patients in Kenya.

Just imagine what could happen as we move beyond such "push" approaches to preventive care? Already 70% of US adults track their health in some manner (e.g., using a Fitbit), and 46% of them say that it has changed their overall approach to maintaining their health or the health of someone for whom they provide care (Fox and Duggan 2013). How might your doctor or insurer use your data to create an incentive for your wellness through either perks for good choices or timely notifications via calls or texts?

Moreover, these tools would offer evidence-based feedback on your diet and activity and provide early detection based on deviations from your baseline health measures.

Data gathering would not be limited to the use of real-time health monitors. Remember your warranty and the regular doctor checkups. Technology poised to augment the old-fashioned blood test could be the model for early

Figure 26. Effects of Text Message Reminders

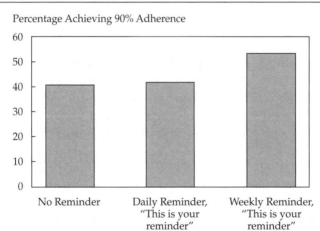

Notes: Text message reminders improved adherence to antiretroviral therapy in a study among HIV/AIDS patients in Kenya. Although reminders have been used for other behaviors as well, especially saving, not all reminders work the same way. In this case, people seemed to tune out reminders that arrived daily.
Source: Pop-Eleches et al. (2011).

stage cancer detection (Soto 2014). The potential savings of both lives and money through early detection is very real.

Like access, records and information would be universal. Out of concern for privacy, medical professionals and researchers would be able to access and search data and information only at an aggregate level and based on specific variables, such as age, sex, bio-markers, symptoms, affliction, income, and ZIP code. Individuals and their doctors would have the only biometric "keys" with which to unlock access to the individual's complete, annotated history.

Now imagine how such data could be combined with technology, such as IBM Watson. Watson, today, is set to track (and learn) the world's published medical information and match it against symptoms, medical histories, and test results to formulate a diagnosis and treatment plan. IBM estimates that a doctor would need 160 hours of reading time each and every week just to keep up (Steadman 2013; Cohn 2013). The potential to improve treatments, lower costs, and make doctors more productive is vast, and it is much more than hope.[63]

#10. Charitable Pools and Tools. A single, societal health care system could also be augmented with a single, universal charitable platform to further leverage medical innovation, reduce medical costs, and counteract the impact of aging. Charitable contributions could be specified in a range of ways:

- As a general or targeted research grant.

- To benefit a specific treatment facility or to ease the affordability of a specific drug or treatment—for instance, the development *and purchase* of orphan drugs.

- As an HSA builder for those in need. Contributions would be for anyone who qualified but could not be limited to any subset smaller than a specific city or ZIP code.

- As a tool to specifically fund medical cures—which reduce expensive, continuous treatments—instead of treatments that only mitigate symptoms.

Conditional upon a given society's tax code, perhaps charitable contributions should have differentiated deductibility (from income subject to tax) in which "greater good"–oriented contributions receive higher deductibility.

A Bit about the Insurer: A Key Player. Although many of the principles stated here refer to "an insurer" as the responsible party for all costs

---

[63]And with the advancement in driverless robo-cars, more people will have greater access to care while still living independently. At the most basic level, these cars will be able to "deliver" people to their doctors' appointments.

above the deductible, I did not define the insurer. The insurer(s) in this scenario could be similar to the insurer(s) of today. We have already discussed a structure in which all individuals 18 or older own their own policy, children are covered through family policies, individuals pass through cohorts as they age, and policies are purchased each year. This one-to-one relationship would continue for life. A policy could be "shopped" as frequently as annually by the individual, and coverage could never be refused. Pricing for individual policies could not be less than 50% of the age-cohort average or greater than 150% of the age-cohort average.

In a unique circumstance, such as the need for an expensive treatment or cure, perhaps the insurer should be able to request a future coverage period (e.g., up to 10 years) with no switching of insurers allowed before agreeing to a the treatment or cure. For example, Gilead's "cure" for hepatitis C has a wholesale cost of $84,000 (in the United States) per person over the course of treatment. That amount (apart from any debate on the $84,000 price tag itself) is a rational investment when compared with the potential long-term cost of no treatment: cirrhosis and cancer of the liver. If the coverage will end in a year or two, however, then an insurer's "investment" no longer makes sense.

As an alternative to long-term insurer contracts, each cohort could create its own "mutual" insurance pool funded by a small incremental percentage of the cohort's insurance premiums. Each cohort could act as a reinsurer or financier for members who experience expensive but cost-justifiable cures or treatments (those that are expected to lower future expected medical outlays for the individual) and recover the outlays ratably over, say, the next 10 years from the individual's future insurers. The important point is that insurers that participate in covering any cohort would need to price such a feature. Also, conceivably, insurance premiums might decline over time in the healthier (younger) cohorts because of the health of the reinsurance pool.

■ *To your health and the health of our economies!* The 10 linked components discussed have the potential to increase wellness, decrease costs, and diffuse the ticking economic time bomb in health care. In fact, the McKinsey Global Institute (Manyika et al. 2015) estimates that health care expenditures could drop 25% by 2025 without any negative effects on outcomes if only some of these principles outlined here were adopted. Let's cure what ails us—sick care policies—and never forget that:

An ounce of prevention is worth a pound of cure.

—*Benjamin Franklin*

Today's Health To-Do's (because you should)

The Chopra Foundation has been collaborating with various academic institutions on how meditation, restful sleep, healthy diet, emotional and social well-being, exercise, breathing techniques, and healthy relationships can change disease-related gene expression (Chopra 2014). These practices can, in turn, dynamically change how we experience health or disease. Following are some important points to start now.

#1. Care for Your Care. After all, it is your body—and the only one you will get.

- The first step is to find a primary care physician, if you do not already have one. Then, see the doctor and communicate fully with that person at the intervals recommended.

- Be an advocate for your care. Your doctor may be a knowledgeable professional, but you are the client and know yourself better. In the United States, for example, you can investigate whether a doctor has received funding from drug companies and find out about his or her prescribing habits,[64] and you can determine how patients or peers have graded doctors.[65] You can also find out whether a doctor has been subjected to any disciplinary actions or lost any lawsuits from the American Medical Association.

- Understand your insurance, if you have coverage, and know your rights and obligations both before and after any treatments or care.

#2. Care for Your Body and Mind. Your health is about your body and mind. Be engaged. What are you doing for each, particularly as you age, as discussed in the prior chapter?

■ *It is your body: Move it (so you do not lose it).* **Table 10** shows a list of health problems around the world and indicates the amount spent on the problem annually. Note, in particular, the cost of obesity. Obesity is one of the top three global social burdens generated by human beings. For your weight and your heart, your intention should be to exercise at least every other day each week, and although more is generally better, five days a week is likely enough. A goal for those times might simply be to sweat—achieve your target

---

[64]See the following ProPublica websites, which are periodically updated: https://projects.propublica.org/docdollars and http://projects.propublica.org/checkup.
[65]See the Best Doctors website at www.bestdoctors.com/about-best-doctors and the site www.healthgrades.com.

Table 10. Obesity Burden, 2012

Selected Global Social Burdens	GDP ($ trillions)	Share of Global GDP (%)	Historical Trend[a]
Smoking	2.1	2.9	↑
Armed violence, war, and terrorism[b]	2.1	2.8	↑
Obesity	**2.0**	**2.8**	
Alcoholism	1.4	2.0	→
Illiteracy[c]	1.3	1.7	↓
Climate change	1.0	1.3	↑
Outdoor air pollution	0.9	1.3	→
Drug use[d]	0.7	1.0	↑
Road accidents	0.7	1.0	↑
Workplace risks	0.4	0.6	↑
Household air pollution	0.4	0.5	↑
Child and maternal undernutrition	0.3	0.5	↓
Unsafe sex[e]	0.3	0.4	→
Poor water and sanitation[f]	0.1	0.1	↓

[a]Based on historical development between 1990 and 2010 of total global disability-adjusted life years (DALYs) lost (Global Burden of Disease database).
[b]Includes military budget.
[c]Includes functional illiteracy.
[d]Includes associated crime and imprisonment.
[e]Includes sexually transmitted diseases; excludes unwanted pregnancies.
[f]Excludes lost time to access clean water source.
Notes: Based on 2010 DALYs data from the Global Burden of Disease database and 2012 economic indicators from the World Bank. Data exclude associated revenue or taxes and include lost productivity resulting from disability and death and direct cost (e.g., for health care and direct investment to mitigate). GDP data are on a purchasing power parity basis.
Source: Dobbs et al. (2014).

heart rate for at least 20 minutes.[66] Although this goal is achievable by most people, you should check with your doctor with regard to any specific do's or don'ts before you make strenuous efforts.

Of the many types of exercise, find the type that appeals to you to make the time spent seem less like torture. Cardiovascular and strength exercises should both be done. For a workout, reduced impact is generally better than

---

[66]As a bit of an "old-school" fitness guy, I am skeptical about the under-10-minute workouts. Regardless, a proper warm-up, workout, and cool-down will take at least 20 minutes.

high impact (i.e., more biking and swimming versus running). Strengthening alternatives to weightlifting include Pilates and yoga. It is also important—especially as one ages—to stretch regularly; pliable muscles help balance, which reduces the risk of injuries from falling (as does good eyesight). And, although massage is beneficial, it is no substitute for exercise—sorry.

With regard to nutrition, we all know we can do better. For those who want or need to lose weight (and maybe all others too), consider a basal metabolic rate test to learn about your appropriate caloric intake.

Another test, through saliva, can show you your endocrinal hormonal levels, which will provide insight into your stress level. Stress, as measured by cortisol levels, is a significant contributor to many health risks. Then, consult with a qualified nutritionist to make this information actionable and useful. Your efforts could be greatly enabled if you track what you eat and drink to "see" the truth about your diet. And remember, "everything in moderation."

■ *It is your brain—use it (so you do not lose it).* Never stop learning (see the next chapter). Education has a significant, positive correlation with longevity. This relationship makes perfect sense because of the stresses endemic to blue-collar or part-time work, which are often the result of low educational attainment (Olshansky et al. 2012).

Make time to meditate.[67] It is okay to be skeptical; I was. The neuroscience research is significant, however, and supports the physiological benefits of meditation.[68] Meditation can raise our awareness and attention and expand choice (by improving the time between a stimulus and your reaction). It can also reduce cortisol levels. For all the documented positive benefits of meditation, there are also reports that show the possibility of negative side effects for a minority of individuals.[69]

#3. Sleep. For both your mind and your body, get the appropriate amount of sleep. According to Xie et al. (2013), "The restorative function of sleep may be a consequence of the enhanced removal of potentially neurotoxic waste products that accumulate in the awake central nervous system" (p. 373). Sleep, literally, seems to clear your mind.

---

[67]*Schedule* time or, like me, you will fail.
[68]See, for example, Chade-Meng Tan, *Search Inside Yourself: The Unexpected Path to Achieving Success, Happiness (and World Peace)* (New York: Harper Collins, 2012).
[69]See https://nccih.nih.gov/health/meditation/overview.htm.

5. Learn to Learn (and never stop)

> Education is the most powerful weapon which you can use to change the world.
>
> —*Nelson Mandela, speech given 16 July 2003*

Nearly 50% of all jobs in the United States (or in any developed economy) run a high risk of displacement or disruption by computerized automation in the coming years (Frey and Osbourne 2013). The reasons are technology, globalization, and what Frank and Cook (1995) call a "winner-take-all society." A second-best farmer may earn only a bit less than the best one, but the inventor of the best gadget, the winner, takes all. As winner-take-all opportunities have risen, job opportunities seem to have fallen. And those "less equal" have allegedly become less motivated to even try. Maybe we should never let go of Mandela's weapon—education.

Frey and Osbourne (2013) wrote about the disruptive potential of computerization and how employment in services, sales, and office and administration support, for example, have a very high probability (> 0.8) of being replaced by technology and are just under half of all employment. This is in contrast to employment in management (business and financial), computers, engineering, science, health care practitioners, and technical industries—jobs that have much lower probabilities of being replaced (< 0.2). Those low probabilities, however, are non-zero.

The good news is that, historically, technology has created many more jobs than it has replaced and has also extended our productive capacity. This pattern may not be repeated exactly, however, if only because of the speed at which work has transformed. The speed of technological advancement and subsequent rates of adoption have created a challenge for educational systems to keep up (to the extent that they even legitimately try). Recent graduates and those who have stopped learning face greater challenges than in the past because of the increase in the technical nature of today's work and the winner-take-all condition. Consider the following:

- Blue-collar employment has been the most affected by technological change in the past, but white-collar workers are no longer exempt from the risks. Moreover, which of these two types of workers could more easily accept lower paid service-industry jobs simply to work? Hint: It is not those who spend beyond their means.

- Education is not a panacea. It has its own serious, unique forms of risk. What if your deep expertise becomes passé? Joseph Schumpeter (1976) taught that capitalism is a force for creative destruction. Some specialists (whom the British philosopher Isaiah Berlin [1953] called "hedgehogs") could ultimately give way to the adaptable generalists (Berlin's "foxes") when it comes to sustainable employment.[70]

As we live longer, those of us who are able will also have longer work lives. Older workers will need to remain competitive with multiple generations of younger workers who are more familiar with present-day technologies. The ability of workers to adapt and evolve in skills and knowledge will be key to maintaining relevance in the global economies of tomorrow.

I repeat: Individual responsibility is the key. For example, if we are to be responsible for our retirement savings, being financially literate can only help (or at least raise the probability of) a successful retirement. In the retirement chapter, I discussed a sovereign DC saving plan that required an investment literacy test to invest beyond intelligently constructed defaults. Regardless of whether individuals would outperform the defaults, market integrity would be boosted. A core requirement of our education system should be that everyone working be financially literate. For example, a sound understanding of credit alone would probably prevent a great deal of unnecessary hardship in households.

So, let's begin to learn and never stop. Learning should begin in earnest with children aged 0–8 years old (LaRue and Kelly 2015) if we ever hope to offer opportunity equality—the platform from which to build and best combat income inequality. Consider the words of James Heckman, an expert in early childhood development and winner of the 2000 Nobel Prize in Economic Sciences, "With the global rise in income inequality, children born into disadvantaged environments are at much greater risk of being unskilled and facing many obstacles in life, which is bad for individuals and bad for societies" (Harms, 2014, p. 1).

Heckman further pointed out that gaps in cognitive and noncognitive skills because of differences in economic and social conditions emerge early and can be traced, in part, to differences in early-childhood environments:

> With smart policies we can arrest the polarization between skilled and unskilled, focusing on early years when change is possible . . . Strong early childhood educational programs can help overcome the gaps and help children become better prepared for success in life. (Harms, 2014, p. 1)

Recall those three critical factors from Chapter 2—a stable home, access to good schools, and proper nutrition—and reflect on how preschools,

---

[70]Berlin was referring to a comment by Archilochus (680 BCE–645 BCE), "A fox knows many things, but a hedgehog knows one big thing."

prekindergartens, kindergartens, and elementary schools might be leveraged to help fill early childhood developmental gaps.

- Longer school days and school years could help with situations in which there is little stability in a home and allow for additional education. Such schedules might also give parents—in particular, single parents—the ability to spend more hours at work, which could, in turn, contribute to greater household stability through additional income. The additional income could contribute to economic growth both today and, as a result of improved childhood learning, in the future.

- To the extent that a school can offer or arrange for food, conceptually, the institution could guarantee proper nutrition for up to 10 meals per week (breakfast and lunch, Monday through Friday). For children without access to proper nutrition at home, this program could be a "game changer" for cognitive growth. Some independent organizations already offer this type of benefit. The Peninsula School Feeding Association in South Africa is a wonderful example.[71] Could (should?) local governments shoulder this important responsibility?

Of course, these ideas presume that all schools everywhere are "good." Sadly, in many localities, they are not. Local governments need to appreciate the importance of their schools for all young children. Do you need to privatize your educational system to help enable such progress? Could a given amount of money spent publicly achieve more if spent privately? Regardless of the answer, we still need to contend with the reality that traditional elementary schools cannot help children below the age of four. These are the circumstances in which the "expanded care" section in Chapter 4 might be able to play a role. **Figure 27** provides a wonderful example of how expanded care can help.

The school years from 8 to 18 are important but much less so than the ages 0–8 and arguably less than the college years, which usually start around age 18. So, off to college we go.

As the costs of a college education have risen and employment opportunities fallen, the cost–benefit ratio for higher education that applied in the past has begun to change for the worse. College degrees still make good sense but just not for all students or in all areas of study.[72] In terms of policy, however, and according to Levin and Garcia (2013),

---

[71]See the description at www.psfa.org.za/who-we-are.

[72]Too many college degrees seem to have become less educational and less rigorous over time (Arum and Rokas 2011). Was the reason to allow more people into universities and sell more degrees, increase the value of graduate degrees, or both and more?

Figure 27. Effect of Early Childhood Stimulation in Jamaica on Long-Term Earnings

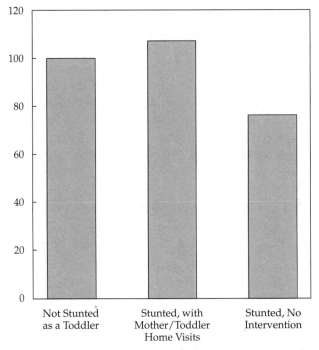

Average Adult Earnings Relative to Earnings of the Reference Group
(those not stunted as toddlers, %)

Notes: A program in Jamaica sought to develop cognitive, language, and socioemotional skills in disadvantaged toddlers. The program of home visits to mothers and their toddlers in Kingston targeted stunted children in poor communities. Over two years, community health aides held one-hour play sessions using a curriculum that promoted high-quality interactions between mother and child. Twenty years later, a follow-up study found that the two-year program of home visits to the toddlers improved long-term outcomes; it closed the earnings gaps between the disadvantaged children and a better-off group. (There is no statistically significant difference between the earnings of the stunted group that received the program and a nonstunted comparison group.) For these disadvantaged children, the program broke the intergenerational transmission of poverty.
Source: Gertler et al. 2014.

There are obvious benefits to the student in terms of better employment and job opportunities and improved options for further education, as well as better health, greater knowledge, and the ability to learn new things. There are also benefits to the taxpayers who pay much of the cost of investment in education. By increasing the numbers and quality of educated persons, society gains from higher economic productivity and income, as well as greater technological advance and inventive activity. Government and taxpayers also experience fiscal benefits in higher tax revenues and lower demand for and costs for spending on public health, criminal justice, and public assistance. (p. 4–5)

Education is an investment and, as such, should offer a decent expected return on invested capital (ROIC). If the ROIC is too low (or negative), college makes little sense. This consequence applies to almost anyone who starts college but does not finish college with a degree.

So, we come to poor educational fit (the gap between types of degrees obtained and jobs available). What does the average 18-year-old know about what she or he wants to do in life? Probably little. How does the average college student's area of study correlate with future employment? Too often, too little. Does it make sense to spend the dollars or take on debt (i.e., invest) to pay for a degree without some clarity on how that investment will ultimately be monetized?

Maybe we need to change the model. The average 18-year-old could benefit from some real-world experience. Nobel Laureate Kenneth Arrow may have given us an answer in 1962 when he wrote that "the pace of innovation is determined within (endogenous to) the model . . . learning by doing." Hmm . . . not all learning is necessarily about college. Consider the following:

- A Brookings Institution report noted,

  Policy and program efforts to reduce youth joblessness and labor force underutilization should focus on the following priorities: incorporating more work-based learning (such as apprenticeships, co-ops, and internships) into education and training; creating tighter linkages between secondary and post-secondary education; ensuring that training meets regional labor market needs; and facilitating the transition of young people into the labor market through enhanced career counseling, mentoring, occupational and work-readiness skills development, and the creation of short-term subsidized jobs. (Sum et al. 2014)

  This approach consists of practical learning, and it is designed to link education to today's job market and to deal with how well the individual fits in a field.

- Some societies place heavy emphasis on experience before university. For example, Denmark requires graduating high school students to work for a year before applying to institutions of higher learning. And in Israel, university students serve in the military reserves throughout their studies. Most go on active duty before or after their advanced studies.

To sum up, real-world experience provides a window into where a young person's interests, passions, and abilities may or may not lie.

According to Vedder and Denhart (2014),

> We now have more U.S. college graduates working in retail than soldiers in the U.S. Army, and more janitors with bachelor's degrees than chemists. In 1970, less than 1% of taxi drivers had college degrees. Four decades later, more than 15% do.

These facts are an indication of the failure of our current educational system. Although computerization, globalization, and immigration have certainly been contributing factors to this failure, poor educational fit has also played a role. Moreover, we must respect that the two proximate recessions in 2000 and 2008 have played a significant role in the severity of this issue.

First Principles for the Educational System

#1. Very Early Childhood Care. First and foremost, we need to care for the needs of our children 0–8 years old as delineated previously. The negative long-term economic impact of children who grow up with less opportunity and become dependent on the social safety-net systems is significant. At the worst end of this spectrum is the risk of criminal behavior and potential incarceration. According to Marilyn Achiron (2014), an editor in the Directorate for Education and Skills at the OECD:

> The metaphor "leveling the playing field" crops up a lot in discussions about pre-primary education. As well it should: attendance in those programs has been shown to improve education outcomes later on. But as this month's PISA [Programme for International Student Assessment] in Focus [Zoido 2014] shows, not even a steamroller can level the playing field of formal education if disadvantaged students are sidelined from the beginning.[73]

Schools in less affluent neighborhoods should start children very young, keep them long into the day and long into the year, and include meals.

Charitable contributions should be allowed that are specific to an individual's education (as with health care). The contributions would have differentiated deductibility, in which "greater good"–oriented contributions could receive higher deductibility. For example, donations toward age 0–8 solutions in less affluent localities could receive a 125% tax deduction whereas all other educational donations would receive only 75% deductibility.

#2. Ensure the Quality of Teaching. Improve the quality of teaching everywhere, for all students. If there is one constant in the world of education,

---

[73]PISA (Programme for International Student Assessment) is a worldwide study by the OECD in member and nonmember nations of 15-year-old students' scholastic performance in mathematics, science, and reading.

it is the importance of teachers. In no way should their importance be underestimated or taken for granted. Eliminating the worst teachers seems to be more important, however, than other teacher reforms. For example:

- The Stanford University economist Raj Chetty (with Friedman and Rockoff 2011) wrote, "Replacing a bottom 5% teacher with an average teacher would increase the present value of student's lifetime income by more than $250,000 for the average classroom in our sample" (p. 2).

- According to University of Chicago economist Luigi Zingales (2012), "Education economist Eric Hanushek has proposed a simple method to improve performance: eliminating the worst teachers. He estimates that . . . the least effective 6–10% . . . would increase U.S. PISA scores by fifty points . . . he also shows . . . such an increase is associated with a 0.87% higher annual GDP growth . . . while Hanushek does not estimate the impact on income distribution of such a change, all the evidence suggests that it would substantially reduce wage inequality." (p. 144).

Thus, teachers must be regularly assessed, held to minimum standards, and dismissed when necessary. Then again, we could be very selective about whom we hire to teach and hire slowly as they do in Finland with great success (McKinsey & Company 2007). Moreover, tenure—that entitlement for teachers—needs to be significantly changed, if not scrapped altogether. Other careers do not have employment guarantees. Regular assessments might best be in the form of a thorough (360°-styled) review from colleagues, parents, and even a teacher's own students instead of solely relying on seemingly objective student test results. Student test results have been shown to be gamed by some teachers and even by schools to obtain additional funding.

Removing low-quality teachers is not enough. The high-quality teachers must also be recognized and rewarded for their value.

#3. Affordable Higher Education. No student shall be enslaved by choosing education or by the cost of a degree. Recall from earlier in this book that excessive debt retards family formation and slows economic growth. This principle consists of two aspects: the cost of an education and the form of payment for the education.

▒ *Cost.* Some tuition reductions have already occurred in the United States because of declining enrollments and competitive pressures. Regardless, students still face high costs, the challenge of the (potential) debt burden, and increased postgraduation employment uncertainty. Only time will tell if the tuition reductions will continue, but without major tuition cuts or higher income and much better planning for the less wealthy, the costs of a degree will remain burdensome for far too many.

Not unlike the potential for technology to improve health, tools such as massive open online courses (MOOCs) could become game changers for higher education costs. The potential improves if more of them were to offer transferable college credits or if online education were to provide degrees that are broadly accepted in the business world (without the stigmas that exist today). MOOCs currently face low completion rates, however, and do not typically reach people who would not otherwise be "degree bound" (Lewin 2013).[74] The certificate programs available today can help someone acquire a specific skill to advance her or his career but are much less useful to those in pursuit of a degree.

Keep in mind that as more courses become creditworthy and distance learning becomes more accepted, completion rates are likely to rise and the level of ability and preparation of the users are likely to increase. Affordability, class flexibility, and the ability to earn college credits (versus just a certificate) are the keys to this outcome. Degree programs that combine distance learning with in-person attendance are probably more likely to succeed than distance-only curricula. Fortunately, MOOCs are expected to evolve to better fit the needs and interests of students, just as any technology continuously adapts to bring greater value to users (Atkins 2015). **Exhibit 4** compares first-generation virtual learning with potential next-generation virtual learning.

---

[74]MOOCs are not just for skills training (e.g., how to program in C++) or entertainment (TED talks). For example, John Cochrane, a highly regarded University of Chicago professor, offers an online version of his PhD-level asset pricing course at www.coursera.org/course/assetpricing. Perhaps the most popular MOOC in history is the Nobel Laureate Richard Feynman's introductory physics lectures, now almost 60 years old: www.youtube.com/user/FeynmanVideoLectures.

Exhibit 4. Next-Generation Learning

First-Generation Virtual Learning	Next-Generation Virtual Learning
Instructor centered	Learner centered
Voice based	Text based
Small groups	Crowdsourced
Prescriptive	Cocreated
Baby boomer learning model	Millennial learning model
Classroom model for learning	Web 2.0 model for learning

Source: Atkins (2015).

A separate area of promise to help lower college costs is the public/private partnership between schools and industry. These programs already exist but could become more of an accepted norm. Conceptually, colleges are a good place for innovation. Moving more industry research and development to that setting can improve cost effectiveness, make R&D more durable (with less recessionary risk), and enhance students' experience as well as provide students with industry contacts for potential future employment. To the extent that any of the innovations achieve market success, the students involved could have their college expenses waived or refunded, and the college itself could direct all remaining profits into the endowment to lower future costs for all students.

▨ *Form of payment.* Freedom from degree servitude may be more easily "solved" through a better form of payment than the current systems. Of course, we could simply make college degrees free and avoid payment altogether. Germany made college tuition free in October 2014. In the United States, according to *Atlantic* reporter Jordan Weissmann (2014),

> The estimated cost to make public, college education free is a mere $62.6 billion dollars! And I'm not being facetious with the word *mere*, either. According to new Department of Education data, that's how much tuition public colleges collected from undergraduates in 2012 across the entire United States . . . The New America Foundation says that the federal government spent a whole $69 billion in 2013 on its hodgepodge of financial aid programs, such as Pell Grants for low-income students, tax breaks, work study funding. And that doesn't even include loans.

By "loans" in the last sentence, he is referring to the same loans that often turn college graduates into indentured servants.

"Free" may be justifiable, but it would need to include trade schools—do not forget the importance of fit—as well as so-called academic institutions. For free tuition to be safe from free riders and to encourage genuine appreciation, let's add a few requirements to help ensure beneficial alignment with the "investors" (that is, with society). Consider vouchers.

- *Nontransferable vouchers* (for all of or part of full tuition), good for a year of education, would be available to all individuals who are at least 18 years old and are citizens. Vouchers would be granted annually and expire after 12 months. Subsequent grants would require that the cumulative grade point average be subject to a minimum (say, no less than a B average). Grants would be usable at any public educational institution.

To help prevent grade inflation or conflicts, better grading systems would be used. For example, as exams become ever more computerized, the questions could become randomized across the students from within a "question bank." All questions could be scored for efficacy and potential review by independent parties to ensure both quality questions and teacher independence.

As an alternative to grades being based on point deductions, grades could be cumulated from the bottom up—based on the number of projects or tests completed during the course. This approach would allow students to *earn* their grades and has been shown to be more effective and motivating than test systems.

After the first granted voucher, a student could receive up to four more, for a maximum of five vouchers. There would be no time limit to use the vouchers, but vouchers would no longer be available once a degree or graduation from a trade school was earned.

Full vouchers would be available for educational paths that address employment shortages in fields deemed by society to be "necessary" (e.g., nurses, physician's assistants).[75] Then, full vouchers would go to those seeking other degrees in science, technology, engineering, and mathematics (STEM) because these fields may be most able to generate sustainable employment opportunities and promote economic productivity. In fact, a report by PayScale and the US National Center for Education Statistics showed that engineering/computer science/math degrees consistently have higher 20-year average returns (best-fit regression of roughly 12%) than arts/humanities degrees (best-fit regression of less than 5%).[76] It is particularly interesting that the returns were relatively stable in both cases across the sample of 240 US universities. What you study—not where—is most important.

Degrees in other areas would be eligible for vouchers, but those vouchers would pay for only 50% of the tuition cost. Humanities and social science degrees have significant value but may offer too low an ROIC to the taxpayer at present to justify tax-supported full tuition.[77]

---

[75]"Necessary" would have to be assessed regularly (i.e., no less than every five years) through employment surveys.

[76]"It Depends on What You Study, Not Where," *Economist* (14 March 2015): www.economist.com/news/united-states/21646220-it-depends-what-you-study-not-where.

[77]Abele (2015) noted that Thomas Jefferson warned about "the drifting from studying the human arts and sciences in academia. Jefferson himself was a staunch supporter of what has been, until lately, the traditional definition of college education. He believed that such studies were inestimable in having a functioning democracy: 'In a republican nation, whose citizens are to be led by reason and persuasion and not by force, the art of reasoning becomes of first importance.' He added to that the critical need for 'an informed citizenry' in the democratic process. As he wrote to his nephew, an integrated, cross-disciplinary college education enhances just that process by providing the skills and information content needed for 'the art of reasoning.'"

Regardless of voucher support, the humanities and social science requirements *for all degrees* need to orient toward communication, collaboration, and problem-solving skills.[78] These three skills—largely outside the domain of specific studies—contain both advantages against computerization and also reasons to be hopeful for innovative productive development. The humanities and social sciences also need to play an expanded role (i.e., no less than a one-year requirement) for all degrees. If the demand for "other," non-voucher-eligible degrees drops as a result of this requirement, we might expect their costs would become more affordable.

With great appreciation that not all individuals are fit for college, 100% voucher coverage should be extended to individuals who gain a "degree" from a trade school. Trade school graduates *can* have higher income, and thus provide higher ROIC to the taxpayer as well as the student, than some traditional college graduates. Voucher coverage could even be enhanced if the individual were to dedicate X years postgraduation to specially designated areas of needed employment, such as infrastructure.

Could this free approach devalue higher education? Maybe. Is free too contentious? Quite possibly. So, let's pursue a better alignment of the incentives with the form of payment. Remember, *individual responsibility* is the core principle of this book. So, who needs to take responsibility—the borrower, the lender, the college, or all three? All three should take responsibility. Although some borrowers (or their families) will always have financial literacy challenges, they are the ultimate beneficiaries of the education. Lenders, for their part, already know better than to lend for degrees that have serious employment challenges or low income potential, and they should behave accordingly; lenders should bear some risk. And the colleges should be responsible for the courses and degrees they offer and for the quality of the education they provide. After all, if a student is unable to find employment after graduation, should the college or lenders not share some of the responsibility?

- *Make the college and the lender into one entity* to remove the problematic third-party payer problem (as suggested for health insurance). The college itself would become the lender to its students and, *voilà*, alignment! Immediately, the challenge becomes apparent: How might (enough)

---

[78]Brynjolfsson and McAfee (2014) wrote, "The innovation scholars… found that the crowd assembled around Innocentive was able to solve forty-nine of the scientific problems which stumped their home organizations for a success rate of nearly 30 percent. They also found that people whose expertise was far away from the apparent domain of the problem were more likely to submit winning solutions" (p. 84).

colleges become sufficiently capitalized and be managed well enough to be the lenders? If a college needed to borrow funds in the short term to maintain operations, then the value of its students' human capital would (essentially) be the collateral. Do colleges increase that human capital, as they should? A corollary benefit of this arrangement could be lower tuitions or at least slower tuition growth rates; after all, tuition has risen over the past few decades largely as a result of the guaranteed third-party government payments.

On the downside, adoption of this suggestion might encourage colleges to offer only degrees that are deemed capable of supporting their creditworthiness and debt repayments (e.g., necessary or STEM-based degrees). On the upside, it would certainly create an incentive for the schools to focus vigilantly on what's best for the students.

- *Adjustable debt repayment.* Let's also consider debt repayment that adjusts on the basis of a student's grade average (e.g., slightly lower rates for grades at or above B and higher rates for lower grades) to align students with their learning outcomes (Arum and Roksa 2011). Some colleges might reduce the variety of degrees they offer, but others might pursue a strategy of offering degrees that attract cash-based students only.

- *Equity conversions* could offer the students (the debtors) some protection. Because quality employment opportunities are not always plentiful for those with degrees, debtors as well as creditors deserve some protection. Lenders should grant an option to graduates for a one-time equity conversion within the first three years after graduation. The option would, for example, convert their fixed debt payment into a fixed equity interest (e.g., 10% of the student's income for the next 20 years). Over time, the highly successful students would be expected to more than offset those who are less successful, if they converted. The indenture risk of those who are less successful would be much reduced, and the college would also be protected. Over time, equity conversions might provide colleges with a form of automated endowment growth such that future tuitions could shrink. Could this free plan naturally increase endowments?

#4. A New Model for Postsecondary Education. For those who are going to pursue college or university studies, the current model of grade school to high school to college needs to evolve. The old mold of college education needs to be broken. One size does not fit all. Specifically, the common step pattern of secondary school to college the next year is not the most intelligent path for everyone (anyone?).

First, for some, college is not a proper fit; a trade school might be better. Think of those intelligent, creative people you know who like to work with their hands. Their investment in a college degree may be of little value to them or society or offer unacceptable ROIC. But do enough trade schools exist today? Are they good? Do enough of the trades offer certificate programs today? If a need for trade schools is not being met, trade schools may represent a real investment opportunity. Perhaps entrepreneurs or benefactors will push the trade school concept further, as Peter Thiel has with his fellowship for students who want to "build something."[79] Such programs offer students hands-on experience—perhaps a better gift than a tuition bill.

Second, not everyone at the age of 18 is ready for college, even if college is the correct and ultimate path for them. The only goal should be a degree upon *exit* from a college; it is not about when the *entry* occurs. Students at Stanford University reimagined the undergraduate system to offer various "pathways" to education and called their platform the "open loop university" (Selingo 2014). Students would enroll and have access to six years of education to use throughout their lifetimes. The traditional pathway—enroll in a residential four-year college and exit four years later with a degree—would be used by only 20% of students today. I was surprised by the Stanford University students' 6-year suggestion and would prefer a 10-year period. Once on a pathway, students could exit at virtually any point or switch directions:

- take a gap-year pathway to collect valuable work experience while trying to figure out what problem they want to solve in life;

- put together a combination work/education pathway in which students would toggle between a campus for a few weeks at a time and a real-world job; or

- follow an easy-on/easy-off pathway from which students might exit 12 or 24 months into the experience to take a job and re-enter a few years later when their skills needed an upgrade, then go back to the workforce and repeat the pathway again.

---

[79]The Thiel Fellowship is described as follows: "Thiel Fellows are given a grant of $100,000 to focus on their work, their research, and their self-education while outside of university. Fellows are mentored by our community of visionary thinkers, investors, scientists, and entrepreneurs, who provide guidance and business connections that can't be replicated in any classroom. With tens of thousands in additional resources, summer housing, regular workshops, our Thiel Foundation Summits, fellowship dinners, and retreats we've built a robust community and program to accelerate your professional and personal development. Rather than just studying, you're doing" (see http://opportunitydesk. org/2014/09/19/2015-thiel-fellowship-for-young-people-100000-grant-for-fellows).

The concept of open-loop higher education fits wonderfully into a continuous, lifelong learning framework, which should be the way that all of us think about education. Imagine the possibility that some years of education could be separated by decades or that new versions of loops could be used by employers for their high performers (as a bonus) or for laid-off workers (for retraining). Once the classic four-year pattern is broken, many new uses for education become apparent. And if we live longer and retire later, we are more likely to have multiple careers, so lifelong learning will need to become the norm.

Education has always been important but never more so than today. Robots have efficiently taken over many mundane, routine tasks and continue to improve even when directed to more varied tasks. The pace of technological progress is such that future human employment needs could become ever more bifurcated between lower-income nonroutine jobs (e.g., hairdressing) and highly technical nonroutine jobs (i.e., those involving problem solving), as depicted in **Exhibit 5**. The routine jobs would be performed without direct human involvement.

Exhibit 5. Routine/Nonroutine Matrix

Cognitive: Routine	Manual: Routine
Falling opportunities	Falling opportunities
Cognitive: Nonroutine	Manual: Nonroutine
Opportunities persisting	Opportunities persisting, but low pay

Source: Acemoglu and Autor (2010).

Notwithstanding the risks of substitution of machine for human being, a robot *and* a human can (and typically must) collaborate, even though we are accustomed to thinking of a robot *or* a human performing a given task. Consider that, as the chess grandmaster Garry Kasparov (2010) observed,

> A weak human + machine + a better process was superior to a strong computer alone and, more remarkably, superior to a strong human + machine + inferior process . . . Human strategic guidance combined with the tactical acuity of a computer was overwhelming.

Might this observation help alleviate some of the fears about robotics? For those situations where substitution is a realistic possibility, other paths toward employability are possible. The following "steps" describe how to start down one of five paths where computers can be augmented by humans (Davenport and Kirby 2015).

- Step up: Lead others, orchestrate the troops. For this step, leadership, among other skills, needs to be developed. Education is needed.

- Step aside: Develop your other intelligences, beyond IQ. Think about how your "people skills" could add value. This step works for those who like to work with or around people. Will introverts be comfortable on this path? Could the therapist or counselor profession offer a path that is safe (yet disappointing because of what it reveals about the need for therapy)? After all, computers do not have empathy; people do not like to interact with them on human-related topics, so demand for help from those who are substituted for machines might be steady.

- Step in: Be ready to monitor and modify the computer's actions. This step is for those who are comfortable with computers. Checks and interruptions will be necessary at times. Think how programmed trading can exacerbate directional moves and sometimes needs to be overridden. Education, STEM in particular, is needed for this step.

- Step narrowly: Computers do not (currently) reside in all spaces. For this step, specialize and obtain education where oceans are blue(r)—that is, in unchartered computer waters.[80] Of course, specialization increases hedgehog risk.

- Step forward: Stay at the cutting edge of technology and applications. Higher education may or may not be needed, but the need to stay educated and current *is* required.

The future will always remain unknown, of course, but continuous education or skills development along the lines of lifelong learning is the single best unemployment insurance policy. Let's become our own safety-net minders. Furthermore, do not become overly discouraged. In the words of Pablo Picasso, "Computers are useless. They can only give you answers."[81] How is that for an example of the value of the humanities? Because innovation begins with questions, the way forward begins with people who understand enough to ask great questions. Let's all learn (more). Just as life is a journey and not a destination, so is our learning. Lifelong learning even offers benefits to retired individuals—to stave off the health-related risks of boredom and exercise the mind, an activity with its own health benefits.

This chapter purposely focused on the structure of educational systems versus the methods within those systems—that is, what works best inside a classroom. Although we must respect those who know and practice the best techniques inside the classroom, the effectiveness of those techniques largely depends on the soundness of the educational system's overall structure.

---

[80]"Blue waters" is a reference to the 2005 book by Kim and Mauborgne, *Blue Ocean Strategy*.
[81]The quotation probably traces back to an article in the *Paris Review* (see Fifield 1964).

Furthermore, because the system serves a public good, it needs to be publicly funded. However, because the quality of the education is paramount, publicly funded schools may or may not mean publicly delivered education. The mode of delivery should be selected in each instance to maximize quality. Finally, vigilance is required to maintain the ethical principles that underlie the "why" of education. As the educational reformer John Dewey (1903) wrote, "School is fundamentally an institution erected by society . . . to exercise a certain specific function in maintaining the life and advancing the welfare of society" (p. 10).

> The most valuable of all capital is that invested in human beings.
>
> —*Alfred Marshall*, Principles of Economics, *2009*

Today's Educational To-Do's (learn 'em, love 'em, live 'em)

Here I summarize things you can do today to pursue lifelong learning: learning how to learn, how to manage costs, pursuing education that is available for free, financial literacy, and a post-secondary-school strategy that inflates your ROIC.

#1. Learn How to Learn. First and foremost, all individuals need to learn *how* to learn. The good news is that tools and techniques are available free of charge on how to learn or learn better.[82] Perhaps even better news is that we have learned that it is not simply about innate talent but, rather, about deliberate practice, in which the technique of how you learn is as important as how hard you try (Colvin 2008; Coyle 2009; Ericsson, Krampe, and Tesch-Römer 1993). Yes, there are those who have natural gifts, but that does not mean the rest of us cannot raise our own games. Have you discovered your gifts? Do you have a mindset that will better enable your game?[83]

Deliberate practice requires emotional intelligence (EI) and resilience (both of which can be developed). EI has been defined as "the ability to recognize one's own and other people's emotions, to discriminate between different feelings and label them appropriately, and to use emotional information to guide thinking and behavior" (Colman 2008), and resilience is essentially the ability to deal or cope with failure or setbacks. When you make mistakes, do you feel angry or wonder why and where you went wrong? What is your attitude

---

[82]See "Learning How to Learn: Powerful Mental Tools to Help You Master Tough Subjects," Coursera, University of California, San Diego: www.coursera.org/learn/learning-how-to-learn; Dunlosky et al. (2013).

[83]See Carol Dweck, *Mindset: The New Psychology of Success* (New York: Ballantine Books, 2007). Dweck also talks about this topic in a video presentation at www.youtube.com/watch?v=-71zdXCMU6A.

toward feedback, which is what mistakes offer us all?[84] If you are open and curious—both learning states—you wonder why when you make a mistake. If you feel angry, then you are closed and defensive—in which states, learning cannot occur. Interestingly, being closed happens when we sense that our security, approval, or control is threatened. The best defense against defensiveness is to simply pause and ask whether it is true that security, approval, or control is *really* threatened at that moment (versus simply a blow to your ego).

Be curious, my friends... or is it too late, and you plan to take a match to this book?

#2. Manage Higher-Education Costs. Unless and until some of the chapter's ideas take hold, the main goal for today is how best to manage costs for those who will attend college. Unfortunately, structural impediments to education are largely outside our control. One example of an exception to this is how a local petition or movement could push for a full-day kindergarten from a half-day schedule.

#3. Go All In for Free Education. Pursue all that is available for free. These offerings may be, but are not exclusively, scholarship opportunities for the few, the fortunate. Can a teenager take advanced placement (AP) classes in secondary school? Can she or he earn college credits for free? I understand that not all secondary students are able to enroll in AP classes, but why not? Let's apply more learning techniques to increase opportunities—such as the "learning *how* to learn" ideas in #1—for all children as they move into their early teens. For kids in secondary school, look to #6.

#4. Achieve Financial Literacy. Considering the importance of finance in all our daily lives, everyone should pursue financial literacy. To begin, let's require such a curriculum in our primary and/or secondary schools. Knowing just the basics of budgets, credit, and insurance before living "independently" post–secondary schooling can be invaluable. For adults, (local) governmental resources are often available to help guide one to unbiased content and online educational (MOOC-style) tools from which to choose. Of course, real-life personal financial situations often differ from what is taught about the "correct decision." The best way to make effective real-life financial decisions is to make and use a financial plan as your guide and purposefully make your financial decisions slowly (to verify resources if need be and to remove at-the-moment emotions). Lastly, some sense of control over one's finances, which begins with understanding, can only help with stress.

---

[84]I have learned much, with great appreciation, about feedback from my partners at Focus Consulting Group.

#5. Follow an ROIC-Inflating Strategy. Everyone who is going to college should pursue a college strategy that maximizes her or his ROIC. If possible, a person should begin a college career with a local two-year (junior) college program that emphasizes liberal arts courses with credits that are transferable to a four-year school. With an associate's degree in hand, the student can enroll in a four-year college (if that fits) that is both reputable and, for cost savings, local (to your state or region) to complete your undergraduate degree.

Research indicates that the choice of undergraduate college matters less than believed (Eide, Hilmer, and Showalter 2016). One study (Hersch 2014), however, has shown that income disparities arise not only from differences in the level of education but also from differences in status associated with an individual's degree-granting college or university. This study is troublesome. It is likely to be correct, but the results may be arising from a form of the prejudice that perverts opportunity equality—just like other biases that affect hiring decisions (e.g., gender[85] and foreign-sounding names[86]). What if we were to push for hiring systems[87] that prohibit the disclosure of applicant names and their schools—for as long as possible during the interview process—for those below the age of 35? Then again, as MOOCs evolve, the concept of a degree-granting entity might change altogether.

Someone who needs or wants to further his or her studies to earn a graduate degree should try to attend the best program, regardless of location. Graduate programs can be the most fruitful of your education investments. This decision is a capital allocation problem: Allocate the greatest amount of your capital to the aspects of your education that add the most value.

Everyone who attends a college or university should also strongly consider work or internships during the college years. Get connections and experience.

Finally, a person who cannot or does not want to maximize that ROIC through a college experience should enroll in a trade school.

#6. Raising ROIC through Online and Other Tools. When MOOCs begin to offer widely respected credits, a person should consider how the credits might be used to raise that ROIC. Consideration should also be given to the effectiveness of e-learning for each type of learning, rather than focusing

---

[85]See Claudia Goldin and Cecilia Rouse, "Orchestrating Impartiality: The Impact of 'Blind' Auditions on Female Musicians," *American Economic Review*, vol. 90, no. 4 (September 2000): 715–741.

[86]See Marianne Bertrand and Sendhil Mullainathan, "Are Emily and Greg More Employable than Lakisha and Jamal? A Field Experiment on Labor Market Discrimination," *American Economic Review*, vol. 94, no. 4 (September 2004): 991–1013.

[87]Before you think meritocracy screens in lieu of résumés are unlikely, consider that firms like GapJumpers (www.gapjumpers.me) are changing this game.

solely on cost–benefit calculations. For example, e-learning works well for formulaic information but less so for negotiation skills.

Other free tools, such as Khan Academy, can expand learning and continue learning throughout one's life.[88] Such learning can begin in primary school, continue into secondary school, and be available for adults who may need to update and expand their specific knowledge. In particular, when used through one's primary and early secondary learning stages, such tools can increase the potential opportunity to take AP classes and earn credits—for free—prior to college.

---

[88]See www.khanacademy.org.

Conclusion: It Is Time for a New ERA of Sustainable Growth

If you do not change direction, you may end up where you are heading.

—*Lao Tzu*

A cautionary statement indeed, because:

The future ain't what it used to be.

—*Yogi Berra*

In 2004, Mandelbrot and Hudson argued that "the foundation" of financial markets needs repouring before any more repairs are done. I argue that the foundation of entitlement policies also needs repouring. Society's policies and goals need to be rethought and rebuilt. Based on the expected (low to negative) rate of growth in the number of workers, greater productivity will be needed to simply maintain current levels of growth. In consideration of agedness (of populations and infrastructures) and current levels of global debt, sustainable economic growth requires more responsibility, more appreciation (*not* inflation), and more policies that encourage productive behavior. Policies that reward paying riders, not free riders, are needed.

Demographics do *not* have to be destiny. Arnott (2015) reminds us, however, that

[d]emographics matter considerably more than most people think they do . . . the highest GDP growth is associated with people aged 20–44. A greater presence of children hurts GDP growth by a small amount. But a greater presence of senior citizens hurts GDP growth by a significant amount because the seniors go from peak productivity to no productivity in a short period of time. (p. 2)

These results are what our policies and experiences to date have produced, and they foretell less growth ahead. But we have a choice. If we are able to raise our productivity and lengthen our productive capacity—which we can do—growth rates can rise and become more sustainable. With greater knowledge and skills and increased health spans, we will have the ability to work longer. Our past does not need to be prologue (sorry, Mr. Shakespeare) to our future, but we all will need to take responsibility to ensure it does not become so.

If any questions remain about the importance of the topics in this book, take a moment to consider **Table 11**, which depicts a survey from around the

Table 11. PEW Global Attitudes: Respondents Answering the Question "Children Will Be _____ Than Parents"

Country	Worse Off	Better Off	Country	Worse Off	Better Off
Africa			*Asia Pacific*		
Nigeria	18	65	China	7	82
Ghana	22	65	Malaysia	12	72
Kenya	32	55	Philippines	29	63
Senegal	36	51	Indonesia	25	58
Tunisia	39	49	South Korea	37	56
Uganda	37	39	Pakistan	30	40
South Africa	40	39	Australia	53	39
Egypt	42	22	Japan	76	15
Median	37	50	Median	30	57
Europe			*Latin America*		
Russia	24	40	Brazil	18	79
Czech Republic	58	28	Chile	13	76
Germany	64	28	Venezuela	21	66
Spain	65	28	Bolivia	19	51
Poland	61	26	Argentina	38	44
Greece	67	21	Mexico	39	44
Britain	74	17	El Salvador	42	40
Italy	73	14	Median	21	51
France	90	9			
Median	65	26			
Middle East			*North America*		
Israel	27	41	United States	62	33
Turkey	43	39	Canada	64	27
Jordan	43	31			
Lebanon	38	26			
Palestine	43	23			
Median		31			

Source: Pew Research Center Q8 (from Kohut and Wike 2013, p. 6).

world of whether people believe their children will be better or worse off than they themselves are.

If you expect children to be worse off than you are, how can you go quietly along the current path?

The goal is to create a virtuous circle—a cycle that continually reinforces counteractions to demographic trends and increases economic growth and productivity. Let's rethink our policies along the lines of how a business develops foundational clarity. It starts with the "mission" (why it exists, to do what), then builds a "vision" (what success would look like, what the time horizon is for success), and a set of "values" (beliefs and behaviors that bring together the people needed to accomplish the mission). Consider these foundational elements for our societies.

Mission: To create policies that enable sustainable economic and personal growth

Vision: Within 15 years, to see increased equality of opportunity, manageable public debt, and productivity-oriented government spending

Values: Although it is impossible to know what would align all of us to the mission, research along these lines shows that four values are vital for sustained personal and organizational success (Lennick and Kiel 2011):

- *Integrity*: Words and actions align, agreements are made and kept.

- *Responsibility*: Behavior is accountable with an absence of blame.

- *Compassion*: People have empathy for others.

- *Forgiveness*: People accept mistakes and move forward—because we are all human.

- And, I would like to add *continuous improvement*: Learning from mistakes (failure is feedback, are you listening?) because personal growth is in all of our best interests.

The values expressed are my first step toward repouring our foundational principles. The foundational principles can start a virtuous circle that will help us achieve our vision of sustainable economic and personal growth. **Figure 28** provides some specifics of the virtuous circle that could result from this repouring.

The ability to change the world's prospects is in our hands. All we need is the will to recognize our present reality and make the appropriate changes. To me, this possibility is why all of us who are able need to learn how to fish. We need to do this for ourselves as well as for those who are unable to fish for

Figure 28. Virtuous Circle

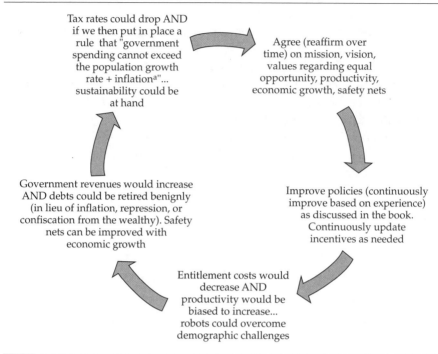

Tax rates could drop AND if we then put in place a rule that "government spending cannot exceed the population growth rate + inflation[a]"... sustainability could be at hand

Agree (reaffirm over time) on mission, vision, values regarding equal opportunity, productivity, economic growth, safety nets

Government revenues would increase AND debts could be retired benignly (in lieu of inflation, repression, or confiscation from the wealthy). Safety nets can be improved with economic growth

Improve policies (continuously improve based on experience) as discussed in the book. Continuously update incentives as needed

Entitlement costs would decrease AND productivity would be biased to increase... robots could overcome demographic challenges

[a]Sexauer and van Ark (2010).

themselves. And for our children, we simply need to do better. Let's start a new ERA of sustainable economic growth NOW.

Mark Twain said, "The man who is a pessimist before 48 knows too much; if he is an optimist after it, he knows too little" (*Mark Twain's Notebook, 1902–1903*). Hmm. I turned 48 while writing this book. Might this year have been the only year I could have written this book?

Appendix 1. Taxes

Consider how simple tax principles might be sufficient:[89]

1. A consumption-based tax should be the core of the system (if savings are good, tax spending) so as to offer an incentive that promotes responsibility.

2. Distinct, additional itemized taxes—for example, to cover safety-net costs—could also be appropriate. In addition, a reasonable property tax might be levied to assist with local government needs. The purposes of any separate taxes levied should be specified; transparency breeds trust.

3. Individual tax exemptions—with household limits—should be included. These could be applied through a tax rebate at year-end (or quarterly intervals if needed to avoid hardship). Society should also discuss whether to "artificially" increase the exemptions for those with incomes below some specified level (i.e., enact a type of negative tax).

4. Additional incentive tax credits could be made available to encourage people toward more responsible behaviors. These credits could be particularly beneficial for those with incomes above a poverty threshold but below society's median income level. Credits should be phased out as incomes reach and slightly surpass the national median income level:

   - Retirement savings credits up to a limit, such as any required contributions (Chapter 3)

   - Health care credits for both coverage costs as well as health savings account (HSA) savings (Chapter 4)

   - Educational savings credits up to a limit, such as 10% of household income

     For all income levels, there should be an earned tax credit for interest payments made on a personal residence up to a per household dollar limit, such as 10× median income. In addition, for those with average and below-average incomes, a proportion of residential rental payments (such as 20%) should be considered eligible for tax credits. Labor mobility among lower-income earners should not be penalized based on whether they can afford to purchase a home.

---

[89]Simple rules are preferred because they make it difficult to game the system or to favor specific interests.

5. Proper estate taxes for estates above $X (forced liquidation of assets should never be driven by a tax) should be included to convey appreciation for what came before and to "pay it forward." This tax would be sequestered (from the government's balance sheet) and used only for programs related to education, health care, or infrastructure (for long-term productivity initiatives). Furthermore, estate tax exemptions might also be earned through "pay it forward" donations during one's life to approved productivity initiatives.

6. Corporations should have a nonusurious (e.g., at most 20% but no less than 10%) flat tax assessed on all profits minus any expenses related to safety nets or benefits. Overseas profits must be brought "home." Of course, it would be important for individual economies to adopt such a tax in unison because it is a global economy after all. All for one and one for all?

Regarding the specific tax rates or limits (consumption, estate, and corporate), we should first try to understand the costs of civilized society before any actual rates are plugged in. Only after such an understanding can a proper dialogue occur and models begin to be constructed in order to estimate the amount of the "need." It is ideal to support only taxes that are sustainable and meet the goals of a civilized society.[90]

---

[90]No "moral code" tells us how much is too much. We should try to avoid the risks (of capital fleeing as a result of taxes that are too high) noted by Jean-Baptiste Colbert (1619–1683), minister of finance for Louis XIV, when he said, "The art of taxation consists in so plucking the goose as to obtain the largest possible amount of feathers, with the smallest possible amount of hissing."

Appendix 2. Dealing with Underfunded Public Pension Plans

Underfunded governmental plans need to make shared sacrifices (i.e., shared responsibility) on the part of pensioners and taxpayers. The assumption here is that underfunded *private* plans can resolve themselves or receive help. Moreover, the services of private companies are generally not as critical as governmental services, such as police and fire.

Pensioner Sacrifice. The liabilities of the promises were (fairly) certain, but the assets, asset growth, and contributions were much less so. At this point, we must consider the following:

- We need to raise the retirement age to some level determined by society, and then, no benefit payments would be allowed prior to that age. For currently retired people, benefit payments would continue unless the pensioner was five or more years younger than the updated retirement age. If five or more years younger, the pensioner could, until reaching the updated retirement age, receive one more year of benefit payments—that is, could receive a type of unemployment insurance—before the benefit payments would cease.

- Benefit formulas need to be updated to be no better than "career average pay, over 20 years." This stricture could include a hard-dollar limit but may not need one. To the extent that any employee contributions existed, the employee would have to be made whole.

- Cost-of-living adjustments, if any, need to be updated to be no better than the national inflation statistic.

- For each year that a "contribution holiday" of 20% or more of the planned contribution was taken, the "then present" plan trustees would need to forfeit 25% of their individual vested benefits.

  - The "then present" legislators would need to forfeit a percentage similar to, if not more than, the plan trustees.

  - We should consider whether the service providers behind the "conflicted" actuarial assumptions (e.g., 8.5% returns) should be assessed a penalty, even if it is only free services for future years.

- Benefit increases in the future would be prohibited, and no new participants would be allowed into these plans. Alternative retirement plans would be made available for participants who had no access to the pension plans.

Taxpayer Sacrifice. It was not the pensioners' fault that they were promised a monthly pension. Often, however, belief in those promises changed saving behavior; pensioners did not save or saved less than they might have without the promise. (And do not discount the pervasive lack of financial literacy.) The bottom line is that the pensioners need the benefit. So, the responsible (local) government or the "next bigger local, neighbor" government needs to issue a long-dated (e.g., 30-year) bond. The proceeds would go directly into the underfunded plan. The bond would be backed by a local real estate tax increase, which would be sequestered for the sole purpose of retiring the bond incrementally as the annual tax payments were made. A tax on real estate is best for such funding because, although no tax is guaranteed to produce revenues, real estate is the best of the worst in terms of the most dependable for revenue. For example, sales taxes affect behavior in such a way that they rarely generate the revenue assumed.

References

Abdul Latif Jameel Poverty Action Lab. 2011. "The Price Is Wrong: Charging Small Fees Dramatically Reduces Access to Important Products for the Poor." *J-Pal Bulletin* (April): www.povertyactionlab.org/sites/default/files/publications/The%20Price%20is%20Wrong.pdf.

Abele, Robert. 2015. "The Capitalist Takeover of Higher Education." Counterpunch.org (25 March): www.counterpunch.org/2015/03/25/the-capitalist-takeover-of-higher-education.

Acemoglu, Daron, and David Autor. 2010. "Skills, Tasks and Technologies: Implications for Employment and Earnings." NBER Working Paper 16082 (June).

Achiron, Marilyn. 2014. "The Socio-Economic Divide in Pre-Primary Education." *Education & Skills Today* (10 June): http://oecdeducationtoday.blogspot.fr/2014/06/the-socio-economic-divide-in-pre.html.

Aeppel, Timothy. 2014. "Economists Debate: Has All the Important Stuff Already Been Invented?" *Wall Street Journal* (15 June): www.wsj.com/articles/economists-duel-over-idea-that-technology-will-save-the-world-1402886301?alg=y.

"Age Invaders." 2014. *Economist* (26 April): www.economist.com/news/briefing/21601248-generation-old-people-about-change-global-economy-they-will-not-all-do-so.

Allen, LaRue, and Bridget B. Kelly. 2015. "Transforming the Workforce for Children Birth through Age 8: A Unifying Foundation." Institute of Medicine and National Research Council of the National Academies: http://buildinitiative.org/Portals/0/Uploads/Documents/Transforming%20the%20Workforce%20PowerPoint%20Presentation.pdf.

Annie E. Casey Foundation. "Early Reading Proficiency in the United States." 2014. Annie E. Casey Foundation (January).

Arnott, Robert D. 2015. "Whither Bonds, After the Demographic Dividend?" *CFA Institute Conference Proceedings Quarterly*, vol. 32, no. 1 (First Quarter): www.cfapubs.org/doi/full/10.2469/cp.v32.n1.4.

Arnott, Robert D., and Anne Casscells. 2003. "Demographics and Capital Market Returns." *Financial Analysts Journal*, vol. 59, no. 2 (March/April): 20–29.

Arnott, Robert D., and Denis B. Chaves. 2012. "Demographic Changes, Financial Markets, and the Economy." *Financial Analysts Journal*, vol. 68, no. 1 (January/February): 23–46.

Arrow, Kenneth J. 1962. "The Economic Implications of Learning by Doing." *Review of Economic Studies*, vol. 29, no. 3 (June): 155–173.

Arum, Richard, and Josipa Roksa. 2011. *Academically Adrift: Limited Learning on College Campuses*. Chicago: University of Chicago Press.

Atkins, Andrew. 2015. "Introducing Next-Generation Virtual Learning." *Rotman Magazine* (Spring): 124–127.

Baumeister, Roy F., and John Tierney. 2012. *Willpower: Rediscovering the Greatest Human Strength*. London: Penguin Books.

Bellucksept, Pam. 2014. "Panel Urges Overhauling Health Care at End of Life." *New York Times* (17 September): A17.

Benz, Christine. 2014. "50 Must-Know Statistics about Long-Term Care." Morningstar (27 July): http://ibd.morningstar.com/article/article.asp?id=657890&CN=brf295,http://ibd.morningstar.com/archive/archive.asp?inputs=days=14;frmtId=12,%20brf295.

Berlin, Isaiah. 1953. *The Hedgehog and the Fox*. London: Weidenfeld & Nicolson.

Beveridge, William (Lord Beveridge). 1948. "Voluntary Action: A Report on Methods of Social Advance." New York: Macmillan.

Blanchett, David. 2013. "Estimating the True Cost of Retirement." Working paper (5 November).

Boult, Chad, Lisa B. Boult, Lynne Morishita, Bryan Dowd, Robert L. Kane, and Cristina F. Urdangarin. 2001. "A Randomized Clinical Trial of Outpatient Geriatric Evaluation and Management." *Journal of the American Geriatrics Society*, vol. 49, no. 4 (April): 351–359.

Boyle, Patricia A., Aron S. Buchman, Robert S. Wilson, Sue E. Leurgans, and David A. Bennett. 2009. "Association of Muscle Strength with the Risk of Alzheimer Disease and the Rate of Cognitive Decline in Community-Dwelling Older Persons." *Archives of Neurology*, vol. 66, no. 11 (November): 1339–1344.

Breslow, Michael. 2012. "Corporate and Executive Spotlight: Michael Breslow, Philips Health Care." Healthcare IT News, video filmed at the 2012 Health Summit: www.youtube.com/watch?v=HvsQdqeXMmw.

Brown, Susan L., and I-Fen Lin. 2013. "The Gray Divorce Revolution: Rising Divorce among Middle-Aged and Older Adults, 1990–2010." National Center for Family & Marriage Research Working Paper Series (March): www.bgsu.edu/content/dam/BGSU/college-of-arts-and-sciences/NCFMR/documents/Lin/The-Gray-Divorce.pdf.

Brynjolfsson, Erik, and Andrew McAfee. 2014. *The Second Machine Age: Work, Progress, and Prosperity in a Time of Brilliant Technologies.* New York: Norton & Company.

Buffett, Warren. 1998. "Buffett & Gates on Success." KCTS/Seattle (May): www.youtube.com/watch?v=ldPh0_zEykU.

Burtless, Gary. 2013. "The Impact of Population Aging and Delayed Retirement on Workforce Productivity." Working Paper 2013-11, Center for Retirement Research at Boston College (May).

Cacioppo, John T. 2010. "Rewarding Social Connections Promote Successful Aging." Paper presented at the American Association for the Advancement of Science Annual Meeting, Chicago (16 February).

Cecchetti, Stephen G., and Enisse Kharroubi. 2015. "Why Does Financial Sector Growth Crowd Out Real Economic Growth?" Bank for International Settlements Working Paper 490 (February): www.bis.org/publ/work490.pdf.

Chetty, Raj, John N. Friedman, and Jonah E. Rockoff. 2011. "The Long-Term Impacts of Teachers: Teacher Value-Added and Student Outcomes in Adulthood." NBER Working Paper 17699 (December).

Chopra, Deepak. 2014. "State of Health: Prevention Is What Matters." *Chopra Foundation News* (25 March): www.choprafoundation.org/health/state-of-health-prevention-is-what-matters.

Cochrane, John H. 2015. "Doctrines Overturned." *The Grumpy Economist* (28 February): http://johnhcochrane.blogspot.com/2015/02/doctrines-overturned.html.

Cohn, Jonathan. 2013. "The Robot Will See You Now." *Atlantic* (March): www.theatlantic.com/magazine/archive/2013/03/the-robot-will-see-you-now/309216.

Colman, Andrew. 2008. *A Dictionary of Psychology*, 3rd ed. Oxford, UK: Oxford University Press.

Colvin, Geoff. 2008. *Talent Is Overrated: What Really Separates World-Class Performers from Everybody Else.* New York: Penguin Group.

Connor, Steve. 2003. "Glaxo Chief: Our Drugs Do Not Work on Most Patients." *Independent* (8 December): www.independent.co.uk/news/science/glaxo-chief-our-drugs-do-not-work-on-most-patients-5508670.html.

Coyle, Daniel. 2009. *The Talent Code: Unlocking the Secret of Skill in Maths, Art, Music, Sport, and Just about Everything Else.* New York: Bantam Books.

Davenport, Thomas H., and Julia Kirby. 2015. "Beyond Automation." *Harvard Business Review* (June): https://hbr.org/2015/06/beyond-automation.

Deevy, Martha. 2013. "Surprising Reasons Boomers Are Working Longer." Stanford Center on Longevity (March 14).

DeLong, Bradford. 2014. "Atrophied Social Network vs. Skill Mismatch Theories of the Unfortunate Shift in the Beveridge Curve: Tuesday Focus." Washington Center for Equitable Growth (10 June).

Dewey, John. 1903. *The Ethical Principles Underlying Education.* Chicago: University of Chicago Press.

Dishman, Eric. 2013. "Health Care Should Be a Team Sport." TED (April): www.youtube.com/watch?v=VT3XyORCFDA.

"Divining Reality from the Hype." 2014. *Economist* (27 August): www.economist.com/blogs/babbage/2014/08/difference-engine-2.

Dobbs, Richard, Corrine Sawers, Fraser Thompson, James Manyika, Jonathan Woetzel, Peter Child, Sorcha McKenna, and Angela Spatharou. 2014. "Overcoming Obesity: An Initial Economic Analysis." McKinsey Global Institute (November).

Dunlosky, John, Katherine A. Rawson, Elizabeth J. Marsh, Mitchell J. Nathan, and Daniel T. Willingham. 2013. "Improving Students' Learning with Effective Learning Techniques: Promising Directions from Cognitive and Educational Psychology." *Psychological Science in the Public Interest*, vol. 14, no. 1 (January): 4–58.

E-Patients.net. "The Patient Activation Measure (PAM): A Framework for Developing Patient Engagement." 2011. E-Patients.net (14 October): http://e-patients.net/archives/2011/10/the-patient-activation-measure-pam-a-framework-for-developing-patient-engagement.html.

Eide, Eric R., Michael J. Hilmer, and Mark H. Showalter. 2016. "Is It Where You Go or What You Study? The Relative Influence of College Selectivity and College Major on Earnings." *Contemporary Economic Policy*, vol. 34, no. 1 (January): 37–46.

Epstein, Gene. 2014. "Work's for Squares." *Barron's* (30 August): www.barrons.com/articles/SB50001424127887323949604580113811574041250.

Ericsson, K. Anders, Ralf T. Krampe, and Clemens Tesch-Römer. 1993. "The Role of Deliberate Practice in the Acquisition of Expert Performance." *Psychological Review*, vol. 100, no. 3 (July): 363–406.

Falk, Michael S. 2002. "Participant Success Hinges on Plan Design." *Profit Sharing* (March/April): 8–10.

Falk, Michael S. 2011a. "Investing, Like Life, Is about Balance." *Defined Contribution Insights* (March/April): 8–10.

Falk, Michael S. 2011b. "Psychology, Neurology… How Your Biology Impacts Your Investment Decisions." CFA Society Chicago webcast (18 May): www.cfainstitute.org/learning/products/multimedia/Pages/59984.aspx.

Ferri, Cleusa P., Martin Prince, Carol Brayne, Henry Brodaty, Laura Fratiglioni, Mary Ganguli, Kathleen Hall, Kazuo Hasegawa, Hugh Hendrie, Yueqin Huang, Anthony Jorm, Colin Mathers, Paulo R. Menezes, Elizabeth Rimmer, and Marcia Scazufca. 2005. "Global Prevalence of Dementia: A Delphi Consensus Study." *Lancet*, vol. 366, no. 9503: 2112–2117.

Fifield, William. 1964. "Pablo Picasso: A Composite Interview." *Paris Review* (Summer/Fall).

Fink, Carsten, Ernest Miguelez, and Julio Raffo. 2013. "The Global Race for Inventors." VoxEU.org (17 July): www.voxeu.org/article/global-race-inventors.

Fox, Susannah, and Maeve Duggan. 2013. "Tracking for Health." Pew Research Center's Internet & American Life Project (28 January): www.pewinternet.org/files/old-media/Files/Reports/2013/PIP_TrackingforHealth%20with%20appendix.pdf.

Frank, Robert H., and Philip J. Cook. 1995. *The Winner-Take-All Society: Why the Few at the Top Get So Much More Than the Rest of Us*. New York: Free Press.

Frey, Carl Benedikt, and Michael A. Osbourne. 2013. "The Future of Employment: How Susceptible Are Jobs to Computerisation?" Working paper, Oxford Martin School, University of Oxford (17 September): www.oxfordmartin.ox.ac.uk/downloads/academic/The_Future_of_Employment.pdf.

Friedberg, Leora, Wenliang Hou, Wei Sun, Anthony Webb, and Zhenyu Li. 2014. "New Evidence on the Risk of Requiring Long-Term Care." Working Paper 2014-12, Center for Retirement Research at Boston College (November): http://crr.bc.edu/wp-content/uploads/2014/11/wp_2014-12.pdf.

Furchtgott-Roth, Diana. 2013. "The Myth of Increasing Income Inequality." Manhattan Institute for Policy Research (16 December): www.manhattan-institute.org/pdf/ir_2.pdf.

G30 Working Group. "Long-Term Finance and Economic Growth." 2013. Group of Thirty (February).

Gawande, Atul. 2014. *Being Mortal: Medicine and What Matters in the End.* New York: Metropolitan Books.

Gertler, Paul, James Heckman, Rodrigo Pinto, Arianna Zanolini, Christel Vermeersch, Susan Walker, Susan M. Chang, and Sally Grantham-McGregor. 2014. "Labor Market Returns to an Early Childhood Stimulation Intervention in Jamaica." *Science*, vol. 344, no. 6187 (30 May): 998–1001.

Graham, Carol. 2014. "Late-Life Work and Well-Being." *IZA World of Labor*, vol. 107 (November): http://wol.iza.org/articles/late-life-work-and-well-being/long.

Guiso, Luigi, Paola Sapienza, and Luigi Zingales. 2010. "Civic Capital as the Missing Link." NBER Working Paper 15845 (March).

Gusland, Cory, Tyler Harshey, Nick Schram, and Todd Swim. 2010. "Consumer-Driven Health Plan Effectiveness: Case Study: State of Indiana." Mercer Global (20 May): www.in.gov/spd/files/CDHP_case_study.pdf.

Hammes, Bernard J., ed. 2012. *Having Your Own Say: Getting the Right Care When It Matters Most.* La Crosse, WI: Gundersen Health System.

Harms, William. 2014. "AAAS 2014: Early Childhood Education Can Pay Big Rewards to Families, Society." *UChicago News* (14 February): http://news.uchicago.edu/article/2014/02/14/aaas-2014-early-childhood-education-can-pay-big-rewards-families-society.

Haub, Carl, and Toshiko Kaneda. 2014. "2014 World Population Data Sheet." Population Reference Bureau.

Hayat, Usman. 2015. "Has Global Debt Become Unsustainable?" *Enterprising Investor* (12 November): https://blogs.cfainstitute.org/investor/2015/11/12/has-global-debt-become-unsustainable.

Helgason, Agnar, Snæbjörn Pálsson, Daníel F. Guðbjartsson, Þórður Kristjánsson, and Kári Stefánsson. 2008. "An Association between the Kinship and Fertility of Human Couples." *Science*, vol. 319, no. 5864 (8 February): 813–816.

Hersch, Joni. 2014. "Catching Up Is Hard to Do: Undergraduate Prestige, Elite Graduate Programs, and the Earnings Premium." Vanderbilt Law and Economics Research Paper No. 14–23 (28 July).

Hoff, Karla, and Priyanka Pandey. 2006. "Discrimination, Social Identity, and Durable Inequalities." *American Economic Review*, vol. 96, no. 2 (May): 206–211.

IMF. 2009. "The State of Public Finances: Outlook and Medium-Term Policies after the 2008 Crisis." International Monetary Fund (6 March): www.imf.org/external/np/pp/eng/2009/030609.pdf.

Inklaar, Robert, Marcel P. Timmer, and Bart van Ark. 2008. "Market Services Productivity across Europe and the US." *Economic Policy*, vol. 23, no. 53 (January): 139–194.

Isaacs, Julia B. 2008. "International Comparison of Economic Mobility." In *Getting Ahead or Losing Ground: Economic Mobility in America*. Edited by Julia Isaacs, Isabel Sawhill, and Ron Haskins. Washington, DC: The Brookings Institution.

Iyengar, Sheena. 2003. "How Much Choice Is Too Much? Determinants of Individual Contributions to 401(k) Retirement Plans." In *Pension Design and Structure*. Edited by O.S. Mitchell and S. Utkus. Oxford, UK: Oxford University Press.

Iyengar, Sheena, and Mark R. Lepper. 2000. "When Choice Is Demotivating: Can One Desire Too Much of a Good Thing?" *Journal of Personality and Social Psychology*, vol. 79, no. 6 (December): 995–1006.

Johnson, Eric J., and Daniel Goldstein. 2003. "Do Defaults Save Lives?" *Science*, vol. 302, no. 5649 (21 November): 1338–1339.

Jorgenson, Dale, and Barbara Fraumeni. 1989. "The Accumulation of Human and Nonhuman Capital, 1948–84." In *The Measurement of Saving, Investment, and Wealth*. Edited by Robert E. Lipsey and Helen Stone Tice. Chicago: University of Chicago Press for NBER: 227–286 (www.nber.org/chapters/c8121.pdf).

Kasparov, Garry. 2010. "The Chess Master and the Computer." *New York Review of Books* (11 February): www.nybooks.com/articles/2010/02/11/the-chess-master-and-the-computer.

Keynes, John Maynard. 1930. "Economic Possibilities for Our Grandchildren." *Keynes on Possibilities*: www.econ.yale.edu/smith/econ116a/keynes1.pdf.

Kim, W. Chan, and Renee Mauborgne. 2005. *Blue Ocean Strategy: How to Create Uncontested Market Space and Make Competition Irrelevant.* Boston: Harvard Business School Publishing.

Kohut, Andrew, and Richard Wike. 2013. "Despite Challenges, Africans Are Optimistic about the Future." Pew Research Center (8 November): www.pewglobal.org/files/2013/11/Pew-Research-Center-Global-Attitudes-Africa-Release-FINAL-October-8-20132.pdf.

Kurzweil, Ray. "How the World Will Change." Genius.com: http://genius.com/Ray-kurzweil-how-the-world-will-change-annotated.

Kuznets, Simon. 1933. "National Income 1927–1932." NBER (June).

Lennick, Doug, and Fred Kiel. 2011. *Moral Intelligence 2.0: Enhancing Business Performance and Leadership Success in Turbulent Times.* Boston: Pearson Education.

Levin, Henry M., and Emma Garcia. 2013. "Benefit–Cost Analysis of Accelerated Study in Associate Programs (ASAP) of the City University of New York (CUNY)." Center for Benefit–Cost Studies in Education, Teachers College, Columbia University (May).

Lewin, Tamar. 2013. "Universities Abroad Join Partnerships on the Web." *New York Times* (20 February).

Malthus, Thomas. 1798. "An Essay on the Principle of Population." London: Printed for J. Johnson, in St. Paul's Church-Yard: www.esp.org/books/malthus/population/malthus.pdf.

Manchanda, Rishi. 2014. "What Makes Us Get Sick? Look Upstream." TEDSalon NY2014 (August): www.ted.com/talks/rishi_manchanda_what_makes_us_get_sick_look_upstream?language=en.

Mandelbrot, Benoit, and Richard L. Hudson. 2004. *The (Mis)Behavior of Markets: A Fractal View of Financial Turbulence.* New York: Basic Books.

Mani, Anandi, Sendhil Mullainathan, Eldar Shafir, and Jiaying Zhao. 2013. "Poverty Impedes Cognitive Function." *Science*, vol. 341, no. 6149 (30 August): 976–980.

Manyika, James, Jonathan Woetzel, Richard Dobbs, Jaana Remes, Eric Labaye, and Andrew Jordan. 2015. "Can Long-Term Global Growth Be Saved?" McKinsey Global Institute Report (January).

Matsui, Kathy, Hiromi Suzuki, Kazunori Tatebe, and Tsumugi Akiba. 2014. "Japan: Portfolio Strategy Womenomics 4.0: Time to Walk the Talk."

Goldman Sachs Research (30 May): www.goldmansachs.com/our-thinking/outlook/womenomics4-folder/womenomics4-time-to-walk-the-talk.pdf.

Mauldin, John. 2013. "The Road to a New Medical Order." Mauldin Economics: Thoughts from the Frontline (5 October): www.mauldineconomics.com/frontlinethoughts/the-road-to-a-new-medical-order.

McCloskey, Deirdre Nansen. Forthcoming. "Measured, Unmeasured, Mismeasured and Unjustified Pessimism: A Review Essay of Thomas Piketty's *Capital in the Twenty-First Century*." *Erasmus Journal of Philosophy and Economics*: www.deirdremccloskey.org/docs/pdf/PikettyReviewEssay.pdf.

McGonigal, Kelly. 2013. *The Willpower Instinct: How Self-Control Works, Why It Matters, and What You Can Do to Get More of It*. New York: Penguin Group.

McKinsey & Company. 2007. "How The World's Best Performing School Systems Come Out on Top" (September).

Mian, Atif, and Amir Sufi. 2014. "The Most Important Economic Chart." *House of Debt* (18 March): http://houseofdebt.org/2014/03/18/the-most-important-economic-chart.html.

Miller, B.J. 2015. "What Really Matters at the End of Life." TED (March): www.ted.com/talks/bj_miller_what_really_matters_at_the_end_of_life.

Mitchell, Olivia S., and Annamaria Lusardi. 2015. "Financial Literacy and Economic Outcomes: Evidence and Policy Implications." Pension Research Council, Working Paper 2015-01 (January).

Moon, J. Robin, M. Maria Glymour, S.V. Subramanian, Mauricio Avendaño, and Ichiro Kawachi. 2012. "Transition to Retirement and Risk of Cardiovascular Disease: Prospective Analysis of the US Health and Retirement Study." *Social Science & Medicine*, vol. 75, no. 3 (August): 526–530.

Moore, Stephen. 2009. "Missing Milton: Who Will Speak For Free Markets?" *Wall Street Journal* (29 May): www.wsj.com/articles/SB124355131075164361.

Mullainathan, Sendhil, and Eldar Shafir. 2013. *Scarcity: Why Having Too Little Means So Much*. New York: Henry Holt and Company.

Neal, David, and Geoff Warren. 2015. "Long-Term Investing as an Agency Problem." WP 063/2015/PROJECT NO. T003, Centre for International Finance and Regulation (June).

OECD. 2014. "Is Migration Good for the Economy?" Migration Policy Debates, OECD (May): www.oecd.org/migration/OECD%20Migration%20Policy%20Debates%20Numero%202.pdf.

OECD. 2015. "Health at a Glance 2015." *OECD Indicators* (4 November): www.oecd.org/health/health-systems/health-at-a-glance-19991312.htm.

Oeppen, Jim, and James W. Vaupel. 2002. "Broken Limits to Life Expectancy." *Science*, vol. 296, no. 5570 (10 May): 1029–1031.

Olshansky, S. Jay, Toni Antonucci, Lisa Berkman, Robert H. Binstock, Axel Boersch-Supan, John T. Cacioppo, Bruce A. Carnes, Laura L. Carstensen, Linda P. Fried, Dana P. Goldman, James Jackson, Martin Kohli, John Rother, Yuhui Zheng, and John Rowe. 2012. "Differences in Life Expectancy Due to Race and Educational Differences Are Widening, and Many May Not Catch Up." *Health Affairs*, vol. 31, no. 8 (31 August):1803–1813.

Peltzman, Sam. 1975. "The Effects of Automobile Safety Regulation." *Journal of Political Economy*, vol. 83, no. 4 (August): 677–726.

Piketty, Thomas. 2014. *Capital in the Twenty-First Century.* Cambridge, MA: Harvard University Press.

Plassman, Brenda L., Kenneth M. Langa, Gwenith G. Fisher, Steven G. Heeringa, David R. Weir, Mary Beth Ofstedal, James R. Burke, Michael D. Hurd, Guy G. Potter, Willard L. Rodgers, David C. Steffens, John J. McArdle, Robert J. Willis, and Robert B. Wallace. 2008. "Prevalence of Cognitive Impairment without Dementia in the United States." *Annals of Internal Medicine*, vol. 148, no. 6: 427–434.

Pop-Eleches, Cristian, Harsha Thirumurthy, James P. Habyarimana, Joshua G. Zivin, Markus P. Goldstein, Damien de Walque, Leslie MacKeen, Jessica Haberer, Sylvester Kimaiyo, John Sidle, Duncan Ngare, and David R. Bangsberg. 2011. "Mobile Phone Technologies Improve Adherence to Antiretroviral Treatment in a Resource-Limited Setting: A Randomized Controlled Trial of Text Message Reminders." *AIDS*, vol. 25, no. 6 (27 March): 825–834.

Porter, Michael E., Scott Stern, and Michael Green. 2014. "Social Progress Index 2014 Executive Summary." Social Progress Imperative: http://bit.ly/1Sbt17M.

Rajan, Raghuram G., and Luigi Zingales. 2003. *Saving Capitalism from the Capitalists: Unleashing the Power of Financial Markets to Create Wealth and Spread Opportunity.* New York: Random House.

Ramey, Valerie A. 2009. "Time Spent in Home Production in the 20th Century United States: New Estimates from Old Data." *Journal of Economic History*, vol. 69, no. 01 (March): 1–47.

Razin, Assaf, and Efraim Sadka. 2014. "Migration States and Welfare States: Why Is America Different from Europe?" *VOX* (1 September): http://voxeu. org/article/migration-and-welfare-us-and-europe.

Reinhardt, Uwe E. 2013. "The Disruptive Innovation of Price Transparency in Health Care." *Journal of the American Medical Association*, vol. 310, no. 18: 1927–1928.

Rho, Hye Jin. 2010. "Hard Work? Patterns in Physically Demanding Labor among Older Workers." Center for Economic and Policy Research (https:// cepr.net/documents/publications/older-workers-2010-08.pdf).

Robinson, John P. 2013. "Americans Less Rushed but No Happier: 1965– 2010 Trends in Subjective Time and Happiness." *Social Indicators Research*, vol. 113, no. 3 (September): 1091–1104.

Romer, Christina D., and David H. Romer. 2007. "The Macroeconomic Effects of Tax Changes: Estimates Based on a New Measure of Fiscal Shocks." NBER Working Paper 13264 (July).

Saletan, William. 2005. "The New 65." *Slate* (22 February).

Sayer, Caroline, and Thomas H. Lee. 2014. "Time after Time: Health Policy Implications of a Three-Generation Case Study." *New England Journal of Medicine*, vol. 371 (2 October): 1273–1276.

Schumpeter, Joseph A. 1976. *Capitalism, Socialism and Democracy*. London: George Allen and Unwin (http://cnqzu.com/library/Economics/marxian%20 economics/Schumpeter,%20Joeseph-Capitalism,%20Socialism%20and%20 Democracy.pdf).

Schwartz, Barry. 2004. *The Paradox of Choice: Why Less Is More*. New York: Harper Collins.

Selingo, Jeff. 2014. "Big Idea 2015: Let's Rethink the Bachelor's Degree." LinkedIn Pulse (18 December): www.linkedin.com/pulse/ big-idea-2015-lets-rethink-jeff-selingo.

Sexauer, Stephen C., and Bart van Ark. 2010. "Escaping the Sovereign-Debt Crisis: Productivity-Driven Growth and Moderate Spending May Offer a Way Out." Conference Board, Executive Action Series (December).

Shonkoff, Jack P., Andrew S. Garner, Benjamin S. Siegel, Mary I. Dobbins, Marian F. Earls, Laura McGuinn, John Pascoe, and David L. Wood. 2012. "The Lifelong Effects of Early Childhood Adversity and Toxic Stress." *Pediatrics*, vol. 129, no. 1 (January): 232–246.

Shoven, John B. 2009. "New Age Thinking." *Foreign Policy* (8 October): http://foreignpolicy.com/2009/10/08/new-age-thinking.

Siegel, Laurence B. 2014. "Two Top Experts Debate the Outlook for Growth," *Advisor Perspectives* (15 July): www.advisorperspectives.com/articles/2014/07/15/two-top-experts-debate-the-outlook-for-growth.

Siegel, Laurence B., and Thomas S. Coleman. 2015. "The Hidden Cost of Low Interest Rate Policies." *Advisor Perspectives* (28 September): www.advisorperspectives.com/articles/2015/09/28/the-hidden-cost-of-zero-interest-rate-policies.

Skirbekk, Vegard, Elke Loichinger, and Daniela Weber. 2012. "Variation in Cognitive Functioning as a Refined Approach to Comparing Aging across Countries." *Proceedings of the National Academy of Sciences of the United States of America*, vol. 109, no. 3: 770–774.

Smith, Yves. 2014. "Are Immigrants Bad for Government Budgets?" *Naked Capitalism* (5 November): www.nakedcapitalism.com/2014/11/immigrants-bad-government-budgets.html.

Smith, Aaron, and Janna Anderson. 2014. "AI, Robotics, and the Future of Jobs." Pew Research Center (6 August).

Smith, Timothy B., Julianne Holt-Lunstad, and J. Bradley Layton. 2010. "Social Relationships and Mortality Risk: A Meta-Analytic Review." *PLoS Medicine Journal* (27 July): 1–19 (http://scholarsarchive.byu.edu/cgi/viewcontent.cgi?article=1093&context=facpub).

Solow, Robert M. 1956. "A Contribution to the Theory of Economic Growth." *Quarterly Journal of Economics*, vol. 70, no. 1 (February): 65–94.

Solow, Robert M. 1996. "Panel Discussion on the Role of Macroeconomic Policy." *Federal Reserve Bank of Boston's Technology and Growth Conference Proceedings* (June).

Soto, Jorge. 2014. "The Future of Early Cancer Detection?" TEDGlobal (October): https://www.youtube.com/watch?v=dm4fvbrMLPw.

Spettel, Claire M., Wayne S. Rawlins, Randall Krakauer, Joaquim Fernandes, Mary E.S. Breton, Wayne Gowdy, Sharon Brodeur, Maureen

MacCoy, and Troyen A. Brennan. 2009. "A Comprehensive Case Management Program to Improve Palliative Care." *Journal of Palliative Medicine*, vol. 12, no. 9 (August): 827–832.

Steadman, Ian. 2013. "IBM's Watson Is Better at Diagnosing Cancer Than Human Doctors." *Wired* (11 February): www.wired.co.uk/news/archive/2013-02/11/ibm-watson-medical-doctor.

Stein, Herbert. 1998. *What I Think: Essays on Economics, Politics, and Life.* Washington, DC: American Enterprise Institute for Public Policy Research.

Stiglitz, Joseph E., and Bruce C. Greenwald. 2014. *Creating a Learning Society.* New York: Columbia University Press.

Strack, Rainer. 2014. "The Workforce Crisis of 2030—and How to Start Solving It Now." TED@BCG (Boston Consulting Group), Berlin (October): www.ted.com/talks/rainer_strack_the_surprising_workforce_crisis_of_2030_and_how_to_start_solving_it_now?language=en.

Sum, Andrew, Ishwar Khatiwada, Mykhaylo Trubskyy, Martha Ross, Walter McHugh, and Sheila Palma. 2014. "The Plummeting Labor Market Fortunes of Teens and Young Adults." Metropolitan Policy Program at Brookings (14 March): www.brookings.edu/~/media/Research/Files/Reports/2014/03/14%20youth%20workforce/BMPP_Youth_March10EMBARGO.pdf.

Temel, Jennifer S., Joseph A. Greer, Alona Muzikansky, Emily R. Gallagher, Sonal Admane, Vicki A. Jackson, Constance M. Dahlin, Craig D. Blinderman, Juliet Jacobsen, William F. Pirl, J. Andrew Billings, and Thomas J. Lynch. 2010. "Early Palliative Care for Patients with Metastatic Non-Small Cell Lung Cancer." *New England Journal of Medicine*, vol. 363, no. 8: 733–742.

"The Psychology of Scarcity: Days Late, Dollars Short." 2013. *Economist* (31 August): www.economist.com/news/books-and-arts/21584303-those-too-little-have-lot-their-mind-days-late-dollars-short.

Thierer, Adam, and Grant Eskelsen. 2008. "Media Metrics: The True State of the Modern Media Marketplace." The Progress & Freedom Foundation (15 July): www.pff.org/mediametrics/Media%20Metrics%20%5BVersion%201.0%5D.pdf.

Urmson, Chris. 2015. "How a Driverless Car Sees the Road." TED (March): www.ted.com/talks/chris_urmson_how_a_driverless_car_sees_the_road?language=en.

Vedder, Richard, and Christopher Denhart. 2014. "How the College Bubble Will Pop." *Wall Street Journal* (8 January): www.wsj.com/articles/SB10001424 052702303933104579302951214561682.

Waring, M. Barton, and Laurence B. Siegel. 2007. "Don't Kill the Golden Goose: Saving Pension Plans." *Financial Analysts Journal*, vol. 63, no. 1 (January/February): 31–45.

Waring, M. Barton, and Laurence B. Siegel. 2015. "The Only Spending Rule You Will Ever Need." *Financial Analysts Journal*, vol. 71, no. 1 (January/ February): 91–107.

Weissmann, Jordan. 2014. "Here's Exactly How Much the Government Would Have to Spend to Make Public College Tuition-Free." *Atlantic* (3 January): www.theatlantic.com/business/archive/2014/01/heres-exactly-how-much-the-government-would-have-to-spend-to-make-public-college-tuition-free/282803.

Wiens, Jason, and Chris Jackson. 2015. "The Importance of Young Firms for Economic Growth." Ewing Marion Kauffman Foundation (13 September): www.kauffman.org/what-we-do/resources/entrepreneurship-policy-digest/the-importance-of-young-firms-for-economic-growth.

World Bank Group. 2015. "Mind, Society, and Behavior." World Bank Group Flagship Report, World Development Report (www.worldbank.org/content/dam/Worldbank/Publications/WDR/WDR%202015/WDR-2015-Full-Report.pdf).

Wu, Sze-jung, Gosia Sylwestrzak, Christiane Shah, and Andrea DeVries. 2014. "Price Transparency for MRIs Increased Use of Less Costly Providers and Triggered Provider Competition." *Health Affairs*, vol. 33, no. 8 (August): 1391–1398 (www.acr.org/~/media/ACR/Documents/PDF/Membership/RFS/Journal%20Club/Health%20Affairs%20%20Price%20Transparency%20For%20MRIs.pdf).

Xie, Lulu, Hongyi Kang, Qiwu Xu, Michael J. Chen, Yonghong Liao, Meenakshisundaram Thiyagarajan, John O'Donnell, Daniel J. Christensen, Charles Nicholson, Jeffrey J. Iliff, Takahiro Takano, Rashid Deane, and Maiken Nedergaard. 2013. "Sleep Drives Metabolite Clearance from the Adult Brain." *Science*, vol. 342, no. 6156 (October): 373–377.

Yang, Dennis Tao, Junsen Zhang, and Shaojie Zhou. 2011. "Why Are Savings Rates So High in China?" NBER Working Paper 16771 (February).

Yu, Lei, Patricia A. Boyle, Robert S. Wilson, Steven R. Levine, Julie A. Schneider, and David A. Bennett. 2015. "Purpose in Life and Cerebral Infarcts in Community-Dwelling Older People." *Stroke*, vol. 46, no. 4 (April): 1071–1076.

Zingales, Luigi. 2012. *A Capitalism for the People: Recapturing the Lost Genius of American Prosperity*. New York: Basic Books.

Zoido, Pablo. 2014. "Does Pre-Primary Education Reach Those Who Need It Most?" PISA in FOCUS 40, OECD (6 June): www.oecd.org/pisa/pisaproducts/pisainfocus/pisa-in-focus-n40-(eng)-final.pdf.

Zumbrun, Josh. 2014. "The Richer You Are the Older You'll Get." *Wall Street Journal* (18 April): http://blogs.wsj.com/economics/2014/04/18/the-richer-you-are-the-older-youll-get.

RESEARCH FOUNDATION
CONTRIBUTION FORM

☑ **Yes**, I want the Research Foundation to continue to fund innovative research that advances the investment management profession. Please accept my tax-deductible contribution at the following level:

Thought Leadership Circle..................... US$1,000,000 or more
Named Endowment .... US$100,000 to US$999,999
Research Fellow .... US$10,000 to US$99,999
Contributing Donor............................US$1,000 to US$9,999
Friend .... Up to US$999

I would like to donate US$ _____.

☐ My check is enclosed (payable to the CFA Institute Research Foundation).
☐ I would like to donate appreciated securities (send me information).
☐ Please charge my donation to my credit card.
　　　　　　☐ VISA　☐ MC　☐ Amex　☐ Diners

Card Number

____/____   _____
Expiration Date   Name on card   PLEASE PRINT
☐ Corporate Card
☐ Personal Card   _____
　　　　　　　　　　　　　　　　　　Signature

☐ This is a pledge. Please bill me for my donation of US$_____
☐ I would like recognition of my donation to be:
　　☐ Individual donation　☐ Corporate donation　☐ Different individual

_____
PLEASE PRINT NAME OR COMPANY NAME AS YOU WOULD LIKE IT TO APPEAR

PLEASE PRINT　☐ Mr.☐ Mrs.☐ Ms.　MEMBER NUMBER_____

_____
Last Name (Family Name)　　　First (Given Name)　　　Middle Initial

_____
Title

_____
Address

_____
City　　　　　　　State/Province　　　Country ZIP/Postal Code

Please mail this completed form with your contribution to:
The CFA Institute Research Foundation • P.O. Box 2082
Charlottesville, VA 22902-2082 USA

For more on the CFA Institute Research Foundation, please visit www.cfainstitute.org/learning/foundation/Pages/index.aspx.